ON TOUR WITH WORLD
BOXING
LEGENDS

Featuring:

Roberto Duran, Sugar Ray Leonard
and **Thomas Hearns**

by **MARTYN DEVLIN**

Typeset in Gentium Book Basic and Knockout

Editing, design and publishing by UK Book Publishing

UK Book Publishing is a trading name of Consilience Media

www.ukbookpublishing.com

ISBN: 978-1-910223-43-7

★ ★ ★ ★ ★ ★ ★ ★ ★ ★ ★ ★ ★ ★ ★ ★ ★ ★

To Phil

This is the story of how Martyn Devlin, an unknown Geordie buried in grassroots Amateur boxing for a lifetime, unbelievably managed to persuade three of the greatest boxers of all time – Roberto Duran, Thomas Hearns, and Sugar Ray Leonard – to the UK to attend dinner show tours he organised for them. The tours were a follow-on from the momentous reunion that Martyn organised between Roberto Duran and Ken Buchanan some 30 years after their controversial world title fight in New York's Madison Square Gardens.

Best of Luck
In Life & Health.

Martyn

★ ★ ★ ★ ★ ★ ★ ★ ★ ★ ★ ★ ★ ★ ★ ★ ★ ★

Acknowledgements

A very special thanks to

Kieran Lawson -
Lawson Photography

Also to

Alan Shaw
- KO Events

Jimmy Patterson

Ricky Turrell
- Artistic Images

Les Clark Photography

Sincere thanks to *Ruth* and *Jay* from
UK Book Publishing for their professionalism

INTRODUCTION

Having been a decent footballer during my schooldays at both junior and senior level and captain of the 1967 St Mary's winning prestigious Bishop's cup team, I first became involved in the sport of amateur boxing by way of a friend called Colin Deans. Colin was a good amateur from a respected boxing family in the town and boxed out of the Jarrow Perth Green club that was only a short distance from where I lived. Colin attended the college where we were both serving our apprenticeships as Joiners although for different companies and he and a few other lads I knew that boxed in the area were always well respected and known for their high level of fitness. Jarrow was a tough working class town in the north east of England where once you entered your mid-teenage years you gained respect if you could handle yourself – especially in any combat sports. I became fed up with playing too much football and had also done some weight training that eventually became boring so I wanted to do something more physical and exciting. It was after attending an amateur boxing show that Colin was on that I fancied the idea of giving it a go with the gloves on. My younger brother Bryan had begun attending the boxing gym a month or so earlier as one of his friends went there. After a few months of training at the Perth Green club gym under the strict guidance of coaches Frankie and Brian Deans and Ken Sayers, Bryan and I made our debuts on the same bill at the Tavern night club in South Shields and we both won points decisions in front of a big crowd that included our proud late father Tom. I will never forget it as when you are having your first contest it is like leading up to a world title fight and I was so confident I sold lots of tickets and invited a lot of family and friends. I recall I boxed a real tough lad from the St Edwards ABC at Whitley Bay called Davy Flynn who, unknown to me, had already had a couple of bouts and rushed out at me from the first bell knocking me across the ring. I eventually settled to use my stiff left jab as that was all I really knew at the time and went on to win a points decision. The following day I felt like a champion of the world but was aching from head to toe and bruised all over my face. I recall going to the gym the following night when my coach Frankie Deans informed me that I had done well but I would be boxing the same lad again next week. I was shocked at this as I was under the impression I would have been given a long rest just like the professionals but was informed that this was the way it was in the amateur game. This time the bout was much closer but once again I managed to edge the decision. Over the next 15 years I went on to box over 80 contests and eventually won more than I lost but was basically just a club level boxer and always fell short when stepping up in class in the local ABA championships. Having said that, one year, 1984, I boxed a quarter-final and semi-final on the same night beating stylist Mark Jordinson from Stockton and then the teak tough Freddie Keelan from Newcastle's West End both on points, but then was well beaten the following week in the light middleweight final by Sunderland's Gordon 'Pedro' Philips who was one of the best amateur boxers ever to come out of the North East. Although Frankie and Brian Deans, along with Ken Sayers, were very good coaches, one of the best coaches I ever had was former top amateur Barry Ahmed. Barry came too late towards the end of my career but could not devote his time because of his work commitments.

After I retired from competitive boxing I eventually became head coach, club secretary, matchmaker, press officer, gym caretaker along with all the other voluntary jobs that go with running an Amateur boxing club at the Bilton Hall ABC at Low Simonside, Jarrow. I had been at Bilton Hall along with my coach Ken Sayers since Ken had formed the club in October 1985. I had previously been at the Perth Green club since 1975 until its closure during 1984, although it has now become affiliated again to the ABA.

To this day I still coach youths at Bilton Hall on three evenings per week, stage three tournaments per season and attend shows throughout the Tyne, Tees and Wear division in the North East of England. Coaching youths still gives me the greatest satisfaction especially when you have taught a youngster from when they first enter the gym until they go on to win their first bout.

Staging amateur boxing tournaments was all part of running a club and shows were a chance for your boxers to perform in front of their home crowd of family and friends. Shows were a headache to organise and over the years I had found that it was best to do things yourself as relying on others did not work. Once you had your show date set and chosen your venue you had to start with the matchmaking. Matchmaking was one of the hardest jobs in boxing, especially in the amateurs as schoolboy and youth boxers must be within a year of each other's age, within a couple of kilos of each other in weight and evenly matched by way of their experience. Matching senior boxers was easier as once they were 17 they could box someone up to 34 (recent rule changes under AIBA have now made this from 18 to 40). Most matchmakers would tell a few white lies about their boxers to try and get the edge for a win, but over the years you find them all out. I would personally always try and take a look at potential opponents in contest before matching your boxer with them, to be on the safe side. The problem was you could match all of your bouts up which was usually about 15 for your show and then you could lose half of the bouts within a few days of your show due to injuries or what is known in the trade as "he's bottled" which meant that nerves had got the better of the boxer and he did not want to box once show time came. Once you had made your bouts up all you could do was hope everyone turned up. I used to always tell clubs to bring a few spare boxers with them as what you could lose in bouts on the night, you could maybe make up out of the spares available.

The cost of staging an amateur show was always on the increase, so much so that a lot of clubs got to the point where they did not even bother putting shows on because of the work involved and the fear that you could run at a financial loss – so you had to make sure to sell tickets to cover the cost or have sponsorship which was always getting harder due to the tough economic climate. Along with matching your boxers you then had to organise a venue, have permits in place, doctor, paramedic, ring-hire, officials, trophies, meals for boxers, meals for officials, security, photographer, someone to play music fanfares, raffle prizes, make sure strips, gloves and head-guards were in place, scales, tickets, posters and programmes and have all of this ready before the show started.

As another fundraiser, I started staging sporting dinner evenings at which you would feature a former boxing champion as guest speaker. This was a lot easier to do than your tournament show and you had the chance to mix with some of the sports legends, so this was something that I began to enjoy. The biggest concern here was that you had to sell tickets to cover the cost of your speaker and obviously the bigger the name the bigger the fee. I recall one of the early shows I staged ran at a big loss because the show date clashed with a rearranged Sky Sports Newcastle United football match. These rescheduled dates are out of your control and the show ticket sales slumped. I was informed by the community centre management at that time, that if I staged anymore of these dinner shows I would have to finance them myself, so I then decided to go ahead with these shows under the 'Fighting Talk' banner. Over the years I have featured at functions some of the biggest names in British boxing such as Ricky Hatton, Joe Calzaghe, Frank Bruno, Nigel Benn, Steve Collins, Chris Eubank, Frank Bruno, Barry McGuigan, the late Sir Henry Cooper, John Conteh, John H Stracey, Alan Minter, Glenn McCrory and Jim Watt.

Then out of the blue I was given the opportunity to feature a real world boxing legend in Roberto 'Hands of Stone' Duran.

MARTYN IN CORNER WITH STEVEN HALL, 1985

ROBERTO 'HANDS OF STONE' DURAN

Roberto Duran Samaniego was born on 16 May 1951 in the slum area of El Chorrillo, Panama. Abandoned by his father Margarito Duran at an early age Roberto helped his mother Clara and brothers and sisters survive by doing various jobs on the streets that included shoe shining, selling papers, painting, and any other odd jobs at which he could earn money to support his family. Roberto first went to the local boxing gym aged eight and had his first fight a year later. Roberto had only a reported 29 amateur bouts but when he found out he could get paid money for fighting he turned professional aged 16. In a career that would span five decades, Roberto won world titles in four different weight divisions and ended with an amazing record of 120 bouts, 104 wins, and scored 69 KOs.

At the age of 21 Roberto Duran won his first World title on 26 June 1972 when he bludgeoned the lightweight title from Scotland's Ken Buchanan at Madison Square Gardens, New York. The referee stopped the contest after 13 rounds when Buchanan would not fight on after complaining of a low blow although Duran was ahead at the time. Duran successfully defended his lightweight title until he literally fought himself out of opposition.

He held the title for six years defending it no fewer than 12 times, knocking out 11 of his challengers to make the title his own.

Forced to keep busy between title fights he fought an incredible 26 non-title bouts during his reign, relinquishing the title in 1979 when he had clearly run out of lightweights to fight. Today those non-title bouts would possibly have been sanctioned as legitimate title fights giving him an unbeatable record of over 30 successful title defences.

Being able to put on weight very easily Duran missed out the light welterweight division and moved up a full stone to the welterweight division to challenge the great Sugar Ray Leonard who was at that time America's golden boy after winning the Gold medal at the Montreal Olympic Games. At this point Duran had only lost once in 72 fights and had reversed that defeat with a KO win against Esteban de Jesus.

In one of the most anticipated and ferocious bouts ever, on 20 June 1980 in Montreal Duran out muscled Leonard and took the welterweight title from him, but eight months later Roberto was forced into a rematch with Leonard, and quit during the eighth round, as Leonard ran rings around him and frustrated him into throwing his arms up in the air quitting. Although Duran is quoted as saying "No Mas", his daughter Irichelle later informed me that her dad never said that and it was in fact the American TV fight commentator at that time who created the phrase.

After a brief time out of the ring Roberto gradually came back to win the world junior-middleweight title from Davey Moore on his 32nd birthday, 16 June 1983, and then went on to win the middleweight title when he outpointed Iran Barkley in a thrilling contest when he was 38 years old, some 17 years after he won his first world title.

Incredibly in the six years between the 1983 win against Moore and the 1989 win against Barkley, Duran had failed in bids for titles against the great Marvelous Marvin Hagler and Thomas Hearns winning only seven of ten fights in this period.

By this time Roberto was regarded as just a name for the huge middleweight Iran Barkley to destroy, especially as Barkley had knocked out Hearns who was the only man to stop Roberto. His fans feared the worst, yet Duran was able to turn back the clock and out-hustle a much younger and bigger man in Barkley.

Duran would give up his title to take on Sugar Ray Leonard a third time up at super middleweight in an attempt to win a title at five weight classes. Although Duran lost on points Leonard knew he had been in a fight and finished with a cut eye that required several stitches. Roberto gained a moral victory of sorts in that he finished the fight unscathed and redeemed himself from their previous encounter when he had quit.

Another comeback saw him fighting mostly at a lower level for another ten years. Though he lost only seven of a further 26 fights, he always fought to win and you could never quite rule out another surprise performance.

THE CONTACT

Antonio (Tony) Gonzalez first contacted me during September 2000 with regards to whether I might be interested in featuring the world boxing legend Roberto Duran at shows within the UK. Because of Roberto's aggressive and ferocious behaviour in the ring, I had the impression that everybody surrounding him would be of the same calibre.

Tony was the Miami attorney and representative for Roberto and had spotted an advert that I had placed in a boxing magazine that unknown to me also went on sale in America. The advert was for boxing champions that I had featured at my shows who were available for after dinner speaking and appearances at shows in the UK. A few of the British champions that I had featured often rang me up asking if I had any more work for them. Once they had retired from the ring some struggled to get by financially, so I thought it might be a good idea to advertise and see what response came and provide some work for them.

I was at first dubious about the enquiry message from Tony Gonzalez – the very name made me think it could have been the Mexican joker 'Speedy Gonzalez' having a laugh but I checked a few things out via the Internet and rang the British consulate in Miami and had it confirmed that he was Roberto's man, so decided to work on things and give it a go.

Tony Gonzalez was a Miami Attorney at law and a translator for Roberto Duran and came across as a perfect gentleman; he was very professional with his messages via email so I decided to give him a call by phone and have a chat. I got through to a receptionist, who said that Tony was not in his office today but would be in tomorrow, so I left word as to who I was, and said that I would call back tomorrow. The following day I rang again and spoke directly to Tony. He came across as a nice guy and was more than interested in bringing Roberto across to the UK, and he said that Roberto was nearing the end of his career now and that he had never really dedicated any time to meeting his fans

9

in the UK and other countries – but was now prepared to do so. This looked that this could be the opportunity of a lifetime! Tony and I negotiated contracts over several months. American contracts were always a little one-sided so they had to be scrutinised very clearly to make things work. I tried to get some of the bigger promoters in the UK involved but to no avail. They were not interested for two reasons: first they would say the fee was too high and second, and most of all, because they knew Roberto did not speak English, only Spanish. There was also the fear that as Duran gave the impression that he was a wild fiery character, he would cause all kinds of problems and might not even turn up at all.

The bigger promoters in the UK were in the fight game to make a living and any shows that they staged had to be profitable for them without any risks; as Duran brought risks with his reputation as a wild guy they were not interested. I was staging dinner shows because I enjoyed mixing with the champions and listening to tales from the fight scene and as I had my full time day job was not bothered about making a profit from them. I usually broke even but did lose out on quite a few; if any profit was made it was a bonus and I would just put it towards the next show and purchase some new gloves or punch bags for the gym. Shows were always hard to sell being in the North-East of England where the only things that sold really well were football, beer, tobacco, and illegal substances.

Professional Boxing in these parts was pretty flat since the days of Glenn McCrory, Billy Hardy and John Davison, although there had been a minor revival recently. Former Sunderland promoter Tommy Conroy still had his stable at this time but he would always tell me how much of a struggle it was to cover show costs. Most of the newer Promoters would require boxers to sell a certain amount of tickets before they could even get on the bill. Several local lads I knew that had turned professional later regretted it saying they were never paid what they expected and missed all the banter of the amateur changing rooms. To make it to the top in the Professional ranks you had to be special, have a punch, but most of all... be able to sell lots of tickets otherwise Promoters would not be interested in you. What used to amaze me was that a few hundred yards up the road from where I would stage my shows Newcastle United football team would be guaranteed to put in 50,000 fans at each home game, and I would struggle to put a few hundred into our venue. The media had the kids brainwashed with football and to get a mention in boxing you had to be something really special. You could go through ten pages of football before any other sport was even mentioned in newspapers. I recall my own daughter Joy, who was only eight years old at the time, came home one day from school and said she sits next to a Sunderland footballer. When I asked about this my wife Linda let me know that it was one of the youngsters at the school called Michael McCaffery who had been taken on at the Sunderland football academy, so I suppose she was telling the truth. Newcastle and Sunderland had a lot of youngsters in their football academies from the age of seven, but very few made it all the way through to the first teams.

Now that I was given the opportunity, I wanted to bring this world boxing legend to Newcastle but knew it would be too much to ask for Roberto to come all the way from Panama and Tony from Miami for just one show, so I was working on a way of how to get them over.

After months of trying to get other promoters, both nationwide and locally, involved, I decided to go it alone and reckoned I could stage two shows at Newcastle. Tony eventually agreed to come over for just the two shows at Newcastle only. The fee Duran was getting was probably too much, but I was still confident I could pull it off and hopefully break even and then use it as a pilot to trigger a tour off.

I booked the shows for a Friday and Saturday during late October 2001 at the Holiday Inn, Newcastle, which was the venue that I had used several times because of its city centre location, and the function manageress Janet Jubb and her staff were very helpful and down-to-earth girls.

Tickets for the Saturday show were going ok but I was

struggling like hell for the Friday show. Eventually I had to give in and admit to Tony that I could not sell two shows but only one. Tony was not too happy about this but agreed to come over for one show – for a fee that was not a lot less than they were going to be paid for the two shows.

My hands were now tied: I could do nothing about it as the deposit had been paid, so all I could hope was to try and break even, but the very thought of featuring a legend like Roberto Duran at one exclusive UK show was something in itself.

Earlier in the year I had been contacted by a guy by the name of Gerry Tomlinson who said he was representing Ken Buchanan and said that Ken should be at the shows as he had not met Roberto for 30 years since their world title bout in New York when Roberto took the title from Ken. He tried to negotiate fees for Ken to attend each show, but I said I would pay his expenses and accommodate him but that was all.

Gerry decided that this was not enough for Ken and said they were not interested, as he had heard that Duran was being paid good money. I don't know where he had got this from but I thought let him believe what he wanted to. After this Mr Tomlinson must have decided to tell the story to the Scottish press.

Later that week I was contacted by several Scottish newspaper reporters over the matter and found out that they love any bad news or conflicts to report on but all I was doing was telling the truth so I had nothing to worry about. The only one who was going to lose out was Ken Buchanan not meeting up with Duran and for what I had offered him. This may or may not have been anything to do with Ken at this stage, as I had only dealt with Mr Tomlinson.

I went on holiday to Florida earlier that year with my wife Linda and daughter Joy and wanted to go down to Miami to take a look at Tony's set up, but never got there due to the long drive and car hire problems as it would have meant I was having to go on our last day on holiday there, but I did call Tony Gonzalez whilst I was over there.

We arrived back home from Florida on 7th September 2001, just four days before the horrific terrorist attacks on the Twin Towers. I sent my message of condolence to Tony and hoped none of his family or relatives were involved.

Back at home my daughter Joy was beginning to take her lessons in preparation for to receive her first holy communion, so we all attended St Joseph's RC church every Sunday to help her prepare. My wife Linda had converted to Catholicism two years earlier of her own choice and being brought up as a catholic I made sure I also attended as I had lapsed for a few years. If there was ever a time to ask for help from up above with my venture, now was the time, and I made sure I always attended mass when I could. I always noticed in life that those who were successful in their chosen profession of sport, politics, music or whatever, always had a strong faith behind them.

In mid-October I was contacted by a Mrs Jackie Warrilow from Birmingham. Jackie's son was a massive Roberto Duran fan and she had booked for him to attend the show as soon as tickets became available. Jackie asked if I had heard about Roberto Duran being involved in a car crash in Argentina? I had not heard anything but received confirmation about it on teletext – apparently it was life threatening as Roberto had punctured lungs and broken ribs.

I rang Tony's office immediately but was informed that he had flown to be with Roberto at the Argentine hospital. I was concerned for Roberto's health but was informed he would pull through and then I admit I felt a little relieved as I thought there was no way he was going to be able to come now so that the show would have to be cancelled and I would get my deposit back.

I contacted Tony who was at Roberto's bedside in Argentina who said that he was not as bad as all reports and should still be able to do the show. I found this strange. So I asked him to send me a press release to confirm that Roberto would still be fine to come to the UK, which he did a few days later, and I passed this on to the editor of the Boxing News.

About ten days before the show date I received an email from

Tony to say that there were now complications with Roberto's injuries as the doctors had found some fluid on the lungs when they checked him out before releasing him from hospital, and would not let him travel. To confirm this he sent me the doctor's report on Roberto... but it was written in Spanish. My pal at work Paul Craney was always one for eating out at restaurants and I recall him telling me about a Spanish one he had been to in Newcastle so he took me there and asked a waitress to translate it for us. The waitress read it out and it confirmed everything Tony had told me and there was no way Roberto could travel.

I therefore had to cancel everything immediately and refund everybody, which was an absolute nightmare. I was very lucky with the hotel as Janet Jubb was very understanding with me although I had not signed the hotel contract.

I contacted Tony who let me know that Roberto was going to be fine but he asked if I would put the show back for a while. I said that this would be no problem and just to send my deposit back over, but he said that the contract stated that the deposit was non-refundable and that I would have to set up another date within six months. I checked the contract out with my legal advisor and he said that Tony was talking rubbish and that he should send the deposit back, but as it was governed by the law of Florida, I would have to go there to challenge it. This meant that the only answer was to reschedule the show within the six-month period as per our contract.

Due to the September 11 tragedy there was also the worry about flights and as to whether they would ever be able to fly over due to the terrorist's attacks.

After several messages on trying to get the deposit back I gave up and had to 'take it on the chin' as they say in the fight game and so rescheduled the date for the one show only. This was to be during March 2002, which was just within the six-month period.

I decided to slightly increase the ticket price and include a three course dinner. This then helped with ticket sales especially to the local businessmen who usually attended my shows and who liked to entertain clients.

Tickets were going but slowly and although I was advertising in the main boxing news I believe punters were still not that sure about Duran coming. (Nor was I!)

"FIGHTING TALK" PROMOTIONS
in association with
BILTON HALL A.B.C.
PROUDLY PRESENT *A SPORTING DINNER*

featuring THE ONE & ONLY
"ROBERTO DURAN"

On **SATURDAY 23rd MARCH 2002**
at **The Holiday Inn (Formerly the Posthouse)**
Newcastle Upon Tyne City Centre
Arrive at 6.30 pm for 7.00 pm prompt start.
(Dress : Smart)
Tickets : £45.00
(Tickets are Non-Refundable except due to cancellation of event)

ROBERTO DURAN AT NEWCASTLE DINNER SHOW TICKET MARCH 2002

THE BUILD UP

As the time got closer I received a call from Ken Buchanan himself saying that he had got rid of his agent and would come down for what I had offered, and asked me to put this in writing to him.

I heard Ken was attending a dinner as guest at Tommy Conroy's boxing show at Sunderland so I went over and introduced myself to him and he came across as a nice guy. Ken said he was looking forward to meeting Roberto. I said to Ken that I knew there had been bad feeling between them and asked Ken to assure me that he would meet Roberto in a sporting manner. Ken very kindly also confirmed this to me in writing.

Tickets really started to move a couple of weeks before show time but they were mainly in twos and threes and small groups of Duran fans.

I was contacted by a Mr Paul Speak who said he was Ricky Hatton's agent and that Ricky would like to be there as Roberto Duran was his hero; I said no problem and told him the ticket price which was only £45. Paul appeared to be taken back by this but I informed him that I would pay a lot more than that to see my hero. Ricky was at the time one of the rising stars in British boxing and a real nice guy and I am sure he would not mind paying out that small amount out of his own pocket to see Roberto.

I was then contacted by a guy from a firm called Otter Telecom who booked eight seats and said one would be for Ricky Hatton so I also informed him of the ticket price that included Ricky's. Another agent contacted me saying he was bringing with him boxers British featherweight champion Michael Gomez and another rising star Michael Jennings, so I decided to put them all on the same table and give them a good spot. A group from Leicester said they were bringing former world title contender Tony Sibson with them as Duran was his hero. So at least tickets were now starting to move.

I still could not believe the lack of ticket sales up here at Newcastle and began to wonder what I was doing wrong but decided that perhaps Duran was not as big over here as I thought he was, and certainly not in Newcastle which was a football city. As the show time came closer ticket sales increased as word got round that Duran was coming, but there were still a lot of doubters.

I was then contacted by Ed Robinson from Sky TV enquiring about doing an interview with Duran. I informed him that I would have to put that to Roberto's lawyer and would then inform him what the fee would be. He said he would have to talk to his boss about it. He then replied to say no way that they would pay anything as they had a strict budget for shows like this and that all they wanted to do was take a few shots of Duran from the back of the room and said that he would give me the unedited tape for myself, as they would only show a few minutes of recording on the Ringside programme. I checked this out with Glenn McCrory who works for Sky TV. I had boxed on a few shows with Glenn in our amateur days and also featured him as a speaker. Glenn said that was correct and that Ed Robinson was ok and just one of the lads who had boxed himself. So I contacted Ed to say that it would be fine to come up to the show, but not to get in anybody's way and at the end of the day it was up to Duran and his lawyer what access they gave him.

I received a message from Tony Gonzalez giving me their flight itinerary for Roberto, himself and an assistant and asking if I had any contact with royalty as Roberto would love to meet any of the royals whilst over here, and asked if there was a way I could be in touch with them, and let them know he was coming over. I was a little unsure about this but let Tony know that this was impossible due to the security surrounding the royals.

Roberto was due in at about 2pm from the London flight and I had him booked into the Copthorne Hotel on Newcastle's quayside with a suite for him and two adjoining rooms.

I went over to the airport at about midday and nervously sat about, worrying if he was going to turn up or not. I contacted the incoming flights from London desk and asked if the three were on board, but there was no way that they would let me know for security purposes. I tried to tell them that I had a VIP coming and if he was not on the flight it may give me time to contact another guest speaker for the show, but still they would not let me know.

I then asked one of the security guys if they could give me some VIP treatment for my guest. One of the guys could not believe it when I told him who it was, Roberto Duran is coming here! He said I never knew anything about it, and then I thought had I advertised enough? My mobile never stopped ringing with calls from fans that were travelling up the country and wanted to know if Roberto was in the country yet and if he was definitely coming to save them a wasted journey.

I let the security guy know that I was not too sure about whether he was on the flight or not from London and if there was any way he could find out for me. He said he would do his best and to give him a couple of minutes.

A couple of minutes turned into about 15 minutes and I then thought the worst. I was parading up and down the airport's entrance and walkways as it was empty, but then out of the corner of my eye I saw the security guy I had spoken to in his white shirt and heard his radio crackle as he was heading towards me. "Mr Devlin," he called out, and as I turned he looked at me and gave me the thumbs up sign, and came and whispered to me that Mr Duran and Mr Gonzalez where the only two on the flight.

A massive wave of relief came over me like I'd never felt before, and as for the third person I was not bothered about and never even asked about him or her, who was apparently their assistant.

The security guy took me through into the private entrance and the plane landed and the exit tunnel was put in place.

After about 50 people came through the door THEN... there he was, ROBERTO DURAN, a world boxing living legend.

THE REUNION

The street fighter from the slums of Panama who had been the first boxer to out muscle and defeat Sugar Ray Leonard and had been involved in so many historic battles with legends of the ring… Minus his goatee beard but with a thin moustache and dressed in a green bomber jacket with a Disney loony tune emblem on the back of it, dark shades and black slacks, followed by Tony Gonzalez who came straight over to me and greeted me with a hug, as did Roberto. I now felt a lot more at ease with myself as a huge wave of relief came over me. Roberto looked immaculate, but with nothing flash about him; he had thick medium length jet black hair and his skin was coloured as if he was deeply tanned.

I took them straight through to the awaiting limousine; Paul the driver kindly opened the doors for us all. Just before he got in an autograph hunter spotted Roberto and he kindly obliged him with a signing, and off we headed to the Copthorne Hotel. I sat next to Roberto in the back of the limousine and commented to Tony how well Roberto looked; Roberto leant over, said thank you and gave me a hug. As we travelled to the hotel he sang and hummed a kind of salsa tune.

I was not sure if there would be any autograph hunters about so I had my brother Bryan and a friend Ged Needham ready to come up for security if required. The young lad at the desk at the Copthorne Hotel check-in seemed to take forever but then we eventually went up in the lift to Roberto's suite and I booked in the room alongside.

I let them settle in first and then asked Roberto to sign the gloves that had been previously signed by Hagler along with a pair signed by Buchanan and then to sign a pair on his own, I took photos of each signing for authenticity purposes. I then showed Roberto the two excellent prints by the artist Brian Meadows that I wanted him to sign, but when he saw them he said "for me" – how could I refuse and not give him a copy of the

Hagler print and the brawl in Montreal print? As Roberto signed I took note of his large chunky hands which had knocked out so many of his opponents and gave him the name 'Hands of Stone' or in Spanish 'Manos de Piedra'.

We then went downstairs into the lounge were we sat and had a coffee and chatted. I received a call from Bryan asking if I needed him to come up but I said it was ok as there were not too many people about although the usual couple of autograph hunters were at the airport and at the hotel. It always amazed me how the hell these people would find out details when I was the only one who knew in advance.

Roberto told me he had eight children and asked me several questions about myself and wondered why I only had one child, so I informed him that my wife and I had tried unsuccessfully for six years and then out of the blue along came our precious daughter Joy who was now nine years old. It was a fine dry day so we went out onto the quayside and stood by the river for a few minutes but Roberto felt the cold so we went back inside.

I kept in touch with my wife Linda who was also staying at the other hotel where Ken Buchanan was booked in and I then thought it would be a good idea if the pair met up at our hotel before the show. The reason being if things were going to go wrong – although I was quite sure they would be ok – it would be better for it to happen now rather than in front of all the fans.

I asked Roberto through Tony what he thought about it and he said it was fine by him. I then called Linda to tell Ken to come down to the hotel and for her to come along herself; she said she would come later.

Roberto, Tony and I sat at a table chatting and then in walked Ken with two other guys.

I personally had a strange feeling run through me, but as soon as they set eyes on each other they hugged and embraced like young lovers – what an amazing sight to witness in front of only four people, and I also realised it was down to me who had arranged this meeting between these two legends 30 years since they had met in their world lightweight title fight at Madison

Square Gardens in May 1972.

Ken sat with us and his company of two companions, rather than the one he had informed me that he would be bringing with him, and he and Roberto chatted about past fighters and their families. Ken insisted that Roberto had grown taller since they last met all those years ago. I ordered a few more coffees as I was now a lot more relaxed; they had both turned up and showed true sportsmanship and were enjoying the reunion.

I was a little annoyed with the Welsh guy that Ken had brought along with him as he started filming with his pocket camcorder which I did not agree with and did think he should at least have asked our permission and did think it was the height of bad manners as he also continued to do this later on.

Linda rang to ask if everything was ok, so I asked her to get a cab down as I thought she should be there – after all, she had put up with a lot over the past 18 months while all the transatlantic negotiations had been ongoing. When she arrived she looked stunning as ever and Roberto and Tony stood up and hugged and kissed her on each cheek, as they were accustomed to doing.

After an hour or so Ken and his company left back for their hotel and Linda said she would also go back to prepare the security staff for the function. Before Linda left Roberto and Tony came over to her and gave her another big hug, and she mentioned to Roberto that we had prayed at church for his recovery to help him make this event happen and I mentioned to him that she was a converted catholic. Tony said that Roberto was also staunch catholic as were most of the people in Panama.

Tony asked me if there were any shopping malls nearby for them to take a look at. As I worked within the largest shopping centre in Newcastle this was no problem, so I quickly ordered a cab and hoped that they would not insist on a limo. The cab arrived more or less straight away and off we went to the Eldon Square shopping centre. I informed a friend on the control security that we would be arriving there shortly just in case Roberto was recognised. I was expecting one of the security guys there as we arrived but there was no one to be seen.

We strolled around the shopping malls with Roberto looking at the jewellery shops which appeared to appeal to him, and Tony translated that Roberto wanted to know why everything was so highly priced over here. I said that from what I knew Britain was one of the world's more costly countries now due to the high level of taxes we paid on goods.

Roberto then said that he was hungry and I wondered where to take him for a snack. Part of the shopping centre is called the Eldon Gardens which is a little quieter and had a nice restaurant café area, so in we went. They took a look at the menu and ordered two big dishes of pasta with coffees.

We then walked down towards the mall exits and Roberto asked me through Tony where he could get a hat to take home. I noticed the Newcastle United shop was still open so in we went and I bought Tony a baseball cap and Roberto opted for a Newcastle woolly hat, and pulled it on immediately as we got outside and strolled down Northumberland Street.

Not a soul recognised him, especially with his woolly hat on. But what an opportunity for a picture for the Newcastle football magazines – one of the world's greatest boxers walking down the city's busiest street with their club hat on. We took a cab at Grey's Monument and headed back to the hotel.

ROBERTO DURAN & KEN BUCHANAN HUGGING AT THEIR FIRST REUNION MEETING AT THE COPTHORNE HOTEL, NEWCASTLE, MARCH 2002

TONY GONZALEZ, ROBERTO, KEN BUCHANAN & MARTYN

KEN BUCHANAN, ROBERTO DURAN AND TONY GONZALEZ

MRS LINDA DEVLIN & ROBERTO DURAN

ROBERTO DURAN SIGNING PICTURE AT THE COPTHORNE HOTEL

ROBERTO DURAN SIGNING GLOVE AT THE COPTHORNE HOTEL

TOP TABLE AT REUNION DINNER SHOW, MARCH 2002, NEWCASTLE

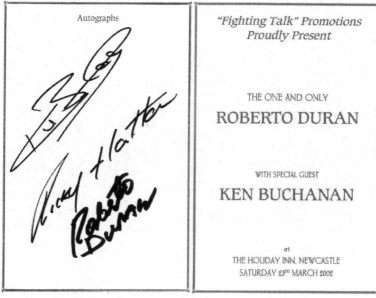

SHOW PROGRAMME SIGNED BY KEN BUCHANAN, RICKY
HATTON & ROBERTO DURAN, NEWCASTLE, 2002

SHOWTIME

It was now about 6pm and the show was due to start at 7 so I had to get a move on. I had a quick shower and took a cab to the venue where I met up with Linda. I realised then that I had left the frames for the signed pictures at home so rang Linda's sister Val and my brother Bryan for him to collect them before he came up; nothing was a problem to Bryan. My phone never stopped ringing all day with calls from across the country from those who were attending making sure Roberto had turned up.

I had met up with Dave Greener, our MC, and briefed him on how I wanted the show to go earlier in the week. Dave was a very good MC; he was a big guy, loud and very professional. He first of all introduced me as the night's organiser and then Brendan Healy, the evening's comedian, and then we welcomed in Ken Buchanan complete with his kilt and trimmings. Ken got quite a good reception but as far as I could gather there were only six Scottish guys in the audience and one of them came with Ken. I was under the impression that Ken would be bringing at least a bus load down from Scotland but I guess I was under the wrong impression.

Dinner was served and we showed big-screen fight clips of Roberto throughout. I had planned to leave for Roberto whilst the stand up bingo was being played and kept in touch with Bryan so that the timing was right. The photographer had not yet turned up and we had a panic on but the lads of Sky TV said that if he didn't show they could help.

I had a cab booked for about 8.30pm to take me down to the Copthorne where the limousine was already awaiting. Paul told me that Roberto was in the bar. I hoped he wasn't hitting the drink but found he was only sitting chatting to Tony and asked for a coffee. I told him that they were nearly ready for us, but he still had a coffee.

Bryan rang to say that the Irish bingo was nearly finished so I said let's go, and off we went to the limousine. The traffic in

Newcastle on a Saturday night is chaos, but Paul our driver took an easier route to the venue; it appeared to take twice as long and I could imagine the audience waiting.

I got Paul to pull up past the main entrance as I had previously set this up with hotel staff to use a side entrance. All of the autograph hunters at the front entrance were a little disappointed, although they may have got a glimpse of Roberto getting out of the limousine. I had, though, informed the Sky TV team what was going to happen and they followed us through to the point where Ian the hotel porter closed the side door on everybody once us three were through.

I wanted Dave to introduce Tony first to make him feel a little special and then hold Roberto back until the fanfare was played.

I chose a unique fanfare that went on for a few minutes as we waited behind the large function room doors. You could feel the tension of the audience waiting to see Roberto. Dave as loud as ever let them have it: "PLEASE WELCOME TO NEWCASTLE THE FORMER LIGHTWEIGHT... THE FORMER WELTERWEIGHT... THE FORMER LIGHT-MIDDLEWEIGHT... AND THE FORMER MIDDLEWEIGHT CHAMPION OF THE WORLD... ROBERTO DURAN." I waited for the fanfare to hit a certain note and then opened the door and let Roberto into the room to rapturous applause. I could feel the room move and of all the champions that I had previously staged, I had never known any of them get a reception like this; it was unbelievable. You had to be there to experience it.

The audience were standing on chairs, tables and anything else they could stand on to try and get a first glimpse of one of boxing's all time greats, the legendary Roberto Duran.

I guided Roberto to the top table were Ken Buchanan was waiting there to greet him. The two legends smiled at each other and hugged with sheer sporting companionship and the tears flowed from Ken's eyes. Dave Greener the MC reminded the audience that this was their first meeting in 30 years and announced that "YOU GET GREAT MOMENTS IN SPORT BUT YOU DO NOT GET MANY LIKE THAT" as the pair eventually let go and sat down next to each other.

Tony took the microphone and said how much of a pleasure it was to be over here and especially to meet up with Ken again after all these years, he then gave the mike to Roberto and translated the Spanish-speaking legend's words of thanks for us having him over here. Dave then went straight into the question and answer session with the fans.

The first question asked was "if it was true about Roberto once knocking out a horse?".

Roberto answered this question for quite some time and told the full story.

He said that he was about 14 at the time and there was a festival going on near Guarare the town where he was born. Roberto was a little drunk at the time and had his eye on several good looking girls. A young guy who also had his eye on the girls challenged Roberto by betting him two bottles of whiskey that he could not knock out a horse that was tethered in the town square. Roberto looked at the girls who turned away from him and said of course he could. His uncle let him know that if he hit the horse hard enough behind the ear it would go down. So young Roberto went up to the horse and punched it behind the ear and down it went, although it was not knocked out. Roberto then went over to his challenger and collected his prize of two bottles of whiskey and then the girls came over and sat alongside him. He then noticed that he has punched the horse that hard that he had broken a bone in his hand.

Dave jokingly said to the audience after the long reply "No more questions about horses please". Roberto was asked the usual boxing questions such as who was your hardest fight? Who do you rate the greatest of all time, and what do you think of boxing now?

One guy stood up and asked why did he not give Ken Buchanan a rematch and Ken sportingly interrupted and said that there was no need for Roberto to answer the question. Roberto was asked if he had seen Ricky Hatton fight. Ricky was sitting at the front table, and Roberto answered with honesty that he had not seen Ricky fight as yet but wished him all the best and told him about the sacrifices that he would have to make to go all the way to the top.

When asked about his heroes he always said Ismael Laguna was the one who'd inspired him most and that Hagler was the hardest puncher he had fought and that his greatest moments were the victories over Buchanan and Leonard, and finally that his wife gave him his hardest fight – that always got him great applause.

After the question and answer session Ken presented Roberto with some whisky glasses from Scotland and Roberto hugged Ken once again and thanked him. He then took the mike and told the crowd about the tribute night that they were having for Roberto in Panama in June and that he would be taking Ken along with him. Roberto had already mentioned this to me earlier in the day at the hotel when Tony informed me that Roberto would be inviting me over there but I thought nothing of it and that he was just being nice at that time.

We then took Roberto up to the photo shoot room where he posed and larked with the fans for nearly three hours. As a gesture I let Ricky Hatton and his group up first and we then called others up table by table.

We held the auction and drew the raffle whilst Roberto was up in the room. One guy bid good money for one glove signed by Roberto; this was gladly accepted. The night's comedian Brendan Healy fell flat on his feet after about ten minutes of trying to entertain those awaiting photos with Roberto, and eventually he held his hands up and gave up realising that there was a legend in the building.

We tried to keep a strict control on the photo session as the memorabilia dealers were out in force trying to bring all kinds of items to get signed but I did get Dave to announce that Roberto would not be signing gloves etc and he would only sign one autograph per person. It worked ok but we still had to keep on top of it as fans were overwhelmed by his presence.

I had the limousine waiting outside as Paul was spot on with his timing and we forced our way through the fans to the limo and off we went back down to the Copthorne. One guy pestered me all night to get gloves signed for his son whom he said had cancer; I agreed to get them done for him later at the hotel. Roberto did them no problem as usual but he struggled with English names for the personal signings, and some were a right mess.

Back at the hotel we went to Roberto's bedroom suite and ordered coffee and steak sandwiches from reception. Tony had invited Ken back to the hotel so he came along with his two guests. We sat and listened to Roberto chat away as usual, and once again Ken's pal got his camcorder out which made me feel a little uneasy but Roberto didn't seem to mind so I thought what the hell – although I still felt it was bad manners.

After an hour or so Ken's party left as I did inform them that we would have to be up at 5,30am for our flight pick up. As Ken left the two hugged again at the bedroom door and once again you could feel the emotion between them. Roberto and I went over and sat at a table near the window and overlooking the river whilst sharing a sandwich on a plate. I said to him Buchanan was crying again and he looked to me and said Duran cry also.

It was about 1am now and so I left them, reminding them we had to be up early for the 6.30am flight back to London.

Once into my room I could hear Tony making a phone call from his room as my room was right next door to his and could not help but hear most of what he was saying which was a mixture of English and Spanish, and gathered it was Roberto's daughter whom he was talking to. The call must have gone on for an hour or so and I wondered how much it was going to cost.

I knocked Roberto up at about 5.30am and gave Tony a call. The limousine was already waiting and once all on board we chatted on the way to the airport about the show. Tony asked if I thought other promoters might now be interested in Roberto, to which I assured him that they now should be. Roberto said to Tony if they were interested I want them to go through Martyn because he is a genuine guy.

At the airport Tony had already checked them in and I walked through to customs with them but could not go any further. As they dashed through to the terminal entrance Roberto stopped, turned around and gave me a huge wave and shouted thank you. I turned back to go to the waiting limo and had a huge lump in my throat. I had done it, featured one of boxing's all time greats at Newcastle and also the reunion with Ken Buchanan.

I went back to the hotel, collected Linda from the Holiday Inn and she suggested that we go to the local Church and thank God that everything had gone ok.

It probably took a few days for it to all sink in, but what made it all worthwhile was the phone calls and emails that I received after the event from all over the country to say how much they had enjoyed the show.

I now had to pay all the bills including Tony's phone bill from the Copthorne which amounted to nearly £500. When I asked at the hotel about this I was informed that hotel lines are always expensive and especially to Panama which was on the charges invoice. I should have challenged him on this before leaving but did not realise it was going to be that much at the time. Anyway the rest of the bills were all paid and I couldn't give a damn about it now – I had succeeded in bringing Roberto Duran to Newcastle, UK for one exclusive show.

The following week I sent over some photos to Tony (well I thought I had due to my inexperience on the computer) and also let him know about the phone bill and awaited his reply.

I had my own problems with the stand in photographer as my regular one was on holiday. He insisted he had only taken 89 photographs on the night and the five door-staff all said it was more like 189 but was definitely more than 89. This annoyed me; we did agree on a percentage of the photo takings and the last thing you want is someone who was a last minute choice trying to slope you and make money for himself on the night. I did check a few things out on the receipt he had given me and yes he had sloped me, not only on the number of photographs, but also by claiming a way over the top processing fee which I found out by making my own enquiries with the shop where he had them developed. I did inform him of this and although he denied it he did come up with some more money but the damage had then been done, and I would never use him again – so he missed out on many more nights over the years with boxing legends.

Mick Worrall, sports editor from the local press at The South Shields Gazette newspaper, attended the show and did an excellent write up about it that I then sent over to Tony Gonzalez. I eventually received an email from Tony Gonzalez thanking me for the time and hospitality that I had given them whilst in Newcastle and asked if I thought the fans might like him to come back again at a later date. I replied by saying that I was sure they would and would start working on a tour as soon as possible.

Tony also mentioned again about Roberto's tribute night in Panama to which he was inviting me, along with my wife and Ken Buchanan too. I let Ken know about this and he asked me to keep him informed, but Linda said that it was around the time of our daughter Joy's holy communion lessons and that she was expected to be with her, for all that she would have liked to go. I informed Tony that it would be just Ken and me who would attend. I was not expecting to hear any more about the tribute night after he'd mentioned it to me in Newcastle but he had stuck to his word.

The date for the tribute night was June 1st, and I wondered how the hell you would get to Panama. I checked this out at one of the local travel agents in Newcastle who let me know that it was quite straightforward. From Newcastle to Heathrow, then to Miami, and then on to Panama – as easy as that. I also checked out the price for a return flight, which to my surprise was quite reasonable.

Ken Buchanan contacted me about the trip and asked me if he was being paid for his appearance in Panama. I thought this was a bit cheeky as I took it that Tony would be paying our travel and accommodation whilst there, and did not think there would be any appearance fee for Ken.

I did not think it was my job to ask for Ken, but he was insisting that he should be paid because I paid Roberto for coming over here, so I said I would ask for him although I did not want to.

As it happened I received a message to say that the tribute night had been postponed until 23 June. I told Ken about this and said I would keep him informed of any definite dates, but did let him know that Tony had stated that there was no fee involved for Ken as it was just Roberto inviting Ken and myself to his party.

I then received a message from Tony to say that the tribute night had been put back again, this time because of the ongoing World Cup football tournament. The date was now set in stone for July nineteenth. I let Ken know about this and once again said that I would keep him informed once I received any flight details.

I reckoned that as it would take a day to get to Panama that we would be leaving on the Thursday eighteenth at the latest and I informed Ken about this. Ken told me that he was appearing in London on the seventeenth so rather than come back to Glasgow he would stay in London.

After trying to contact Tony at his office I eventually received an email in the early hours of Wednesday morning informing me that we were booked onto the 11am flight from London to Miami then on to Panama. I tried to contact Ken first thing on the Wednesday morning but his answer machine was on so I left word on it. I eventually got through to Ken at midday on the Wednesday and confirmed to him that we were due to leave on the Friday and not the Thursday as I had expected. Ken let me know that after talking to his agent he had decided not to go to Panama, the reasons being that it was poorly organised and that he was not getting paid anything for going. I was shocked at this. What an opportunity to visit Panama and be at the party of one of the all time greats with everything paid for; I certainly was not going to miss it. I rang Ken one more time to ask him to reconsider, but once again he informed me that it was too late notice and said that a bricklayer could have organised it better than this, but told me to go and enjoy the trip.

PANAMA

I packed on the Thursday night and set off for Newcastle airport in time for the 6.30am flight to London. At the airport I was informed that a place had been reserved for me to London but no payment had been made. I then checked the follow on trips, and was informed that all flights from London to Miami and from Miami to Panama had been paid for return trips, but not the Newcastle to London. I paid the return flight to London out of my own pocket, as I was not going to miss this for the sake of a £150 flight. I arrived at Heathrow and made my way to terminal three for the flight to Miami. The flight to Miami took nine hours and was not very comfortable, as you are jammed on like sardines on these flights.

Miami airport is not unlike Heathrow, and is massive with thousands passing through of all nationalities, but security was very tight especially after the September 11 saga and I was more or less strip searched at customs. I had to hang around for an hour or so then board the flight to Panama, which was a two hour flight on a much smaller aircraft.

By the time I reached Panama it was about midnight UK time but only 7pm Panama time. I was aware that the show was due to start around 8pm so I knew there would be no hanging around and hoped my pick up would be there at the airport. Panama airport was quite small and dingy in comparison to Heathrow and Miami and there were not a great lot of people around but lots of cab drivers hanging around.

I looked for one of them with my name on their card but could not see anything even close to Devlin. I walked outside to look but nothing, only Spanish speaking cab drivers. Tony had gave me a contact telephone number for when I arrived in Panama, so I went to the desk and asked for them to exchange some dollar notes for cash to use on their telephones which were outside of the building.

The telephones in Panama are completely different to ours and I had to ask a cab driver who was hanging around me muttering some Spanish to me where you put your money in. Eventually I got through only to hear a Spanish speaking answer machine. The time was getting on by now and I could hear Ken Buchanan saying a bricklayer could organise it better than this. I spoke to one of the cab drivers who appeared to be following my every move and asked him if there was anybody there to pick up a Mr Devlin. He muttered some Spanish and shook his head. I then wondered if it had been booked in Ken Buchanan's name.

I then mentioned to him the Roberto Duran show and asked if anyone was booked for a Mr Buchanan. He then went over to one of his comrades and mentioned Duran and Buchanan to him. I was then surrounded by cabbies that were calling out BOOKANAN and wanting to shake my hand. I gathered that Ken Buchanan was still a well known name in Panama as he was the guy whom Roberto had taken the world title from and the Panamanian people obviously remembered the name. I must have obviously had a slight resemblance to Ken, probably caused by my boxer's profile, greying hair like Ken's, similar build and I was white.

By this time it was about 1am UK time and I had been up since 4.30am to be at Newcastle airport, so I was starting to feel a little tired but had to keep awake and get to the venue. I tried to tell these guys that I was not Ken Buchanan but I was wasting my time. I told them I wanted to go to the Roberto Duran tribute night and one of them took me to his cab. As I got in with my case one of the others was banging on the window with a pen and paper in his hand asking for an autograph. I began to shake my head trying to tell him that I was not Ken Buchanan, but then another one came from the other side asking the same. The time was getting on and one of these guys was getting a little angry with me so I thought the best way to get a move on was to sign for them. This I did in my best Scottish handwriting and off we went heading for the Roberto Duran stadium in downtown Panama.

It was about a half-hour drive from the airport with a

Spanish-speaking driver who understood no English at all. The stadium resembled a Spanish bullring, and was surrounded by fencing and fans, touts and armed police. As the cab pulled up several kids and adults came over to see who was in it. The driver lit up a cigarette and told them he had BOOKANAN in the back of his cab. Well word went round again and before I knew it a small crowd had gathered around the cab. I was starting to feel a little apprehensive about getting out of the cab now, especially as a lot of them looked like rouges and I was carrying a lot of dollars and personal items such as flight tickets and passport and I had been warned to be careful whilst in Panama. Eventually a guy dressed in uniform – either police or soldier, I did not know – came over to the cab to see what all the fuss was about and then asked one of his English-speaking comrades to come over to the cab. I explained to him who I really was and why I was here at Roberto's invitation. He laughed and very kindly escorted me to one of the entrance turnstiles and took me through to one of the stewards. I explained to the steward who I was and he spoke to someone on his radio and told me to wait. I stood for about five minutes and then was approached by a broad guy in a suit who took me into the arena.

The arena was circular and huge. There was a salsa band performing on a huge stage with a giant screen on either side and a boxing ring was set up in front of the stage. I was taken to one of the ringside tables, which were plastic, as were the surrounding seats. The guy introduced himself as Frazer and said he was a former Panamanian world light welterweight champion. I could not remember him but took his word for it, as he seemed very helpful. I asked him if there was anywhere I could go to get a wash up and change of clothing as I was starting to feel tired and sweaty.

He told me to follow him and took me across the arena to where the boxers where being changed. Unbelievably this area was also part of the toilet block for everybody and the punters were coming through this area to use the toilets. There were no wash basins or even a mirror on the wall, although there were three frames where they had once been. I asked one of the boxers if I could borrow a towel and I stripped off in the room next to him and rubbed myself down best I could and spruced myself up and then changed into my suit which I felt more comfortable in, although I was only one of a handful that wore a suit that night. As there were no mirrors Frazer straightened my tie up for me and I followed him back into the arena still carrying my case, as there was no way I was going to let it out of my sight.

Two large Panamanians were now sitting at the table along with a guy wearing a white suit and a white Stetson hat with flashing lights on, who came over and introduced himself as Ismael Laguna. This was the former champion of the world from whom Ken Buchanan had won the world title and was one of Roberto Duran's heroes. Then a very tall, elderly chap, well dressed in a check sports jacket sat at our table. Ismael introduced me to him, and said he was Carlos Eleta.

Don Carlos Eleta was the local millionaire industrialist who became Roberto's manager. I asked him about Roberto. He said that Roberto was an exceptional person but it became very hard to handle him, and that he was young and lived life in the fast lane and liked to wine and dine and that he lost control of him and Roberto would only do what he wanted to.

Ismael was a charming man who spoke quite good English; he welcomed me to Panama and asked about Ken and why he was not there. I had to tell him that Ken was not happy with the late notice and that he could not attend. He told me that Frazer was in fact Alfonso Frazer and he had been world light-welterweight champion in 1972.

One of the guys who was sitting at our table was a little deformed and the other was a massive stocky Jamaican who asked me who I was and what I was doing over here. He told me he was a policeman and said he would look after me whilst I was at the event and even for the weekend. I was in a tricky situation so I just agreed with him and said I would speak to him later.

There was a stage with Salsa bands on that were constantly changing and then there was a huge presence of TV crews and photographers and the stadium was starting to fill up quickly. Over to one side of me an elderly lady was dancing to the music and the cameras were flashing around her. Ismael told me that it was Roberto's mother Clara and her sister; he then took me over to meet her. She did not speak English but greeted me with a hug when Ismael informed her that I had brought Roberto and Ken Buchanan together again and was busy organising a tour for Roberto in the UK. I had a photo taken with her and then she hugged me again and asked me to look after her son whilst in England.

The stadium had now started to fill up and you could sense Roberto had arrived. The MC made a few announcements that I could not understand but then the crowd rose as Roberto came onto the centre stage. He was dressed in an immaculate black suit with white shirt and bow tie and looked a million dollars.

A host of champions were introduced on stage including Ismael Laguna, Pipino Cuevas, Ray Lampkin, Vinny Pazienza and a few others whom I had not heard of. They all said a few words and gave the microphone to the MC who then gave it to Roberto. When Roberto has a mike in his hand he likes to keep it and talks non-stop at speed, larking and laughing with all of those on the stage and the salsa performers and the audience – he was unbelievable.

On stage Roberto had all of his family and close friends and then I got my eye on Tony Gonzalez, so I went over to the side of the stage and shouted to him. He immediately turned around and when he saw me he called me up onto the stage and greeted me with a hug and introduced me to all of Roberto's family and the other champions. He then asked me about Ken, so I told him the truth.

Tony then shouted over to Roberto who still had the mike and was centre stage, Roberto looked over and Tony pointed to me and Roberto came over and greeted me in front of the crowd with a hug and put his arm around me and took me to the front of the stage and then rambled on to the audience in Spanish, but I could only make out Buchanan's name and England but whatever he told them received a round of applause. He then passed the mike over to me.

I was shocked at first but when you're put on the spot like that you have to say something. So I just thanked Roberto and Tony for inviting me over to Panama and told them that I had organised the reunion with Buchanan and that Roberto would be coming back to the UK later in the year, and then gave him the mike back as quick as I could. I knew that the majority would not be able to understand me anyway but I received a large round of applause from them.

Tony then introduced me to a few of the other champions who were on stage, including Pipino Cuevas and Vinny Pazienza. Vinny asked if I would be interested in bringing him over to the UK. I said I would talk it over with Tony although I knew he had never really received any exposure over here. Tony let me know that we were all staying at the Ceasar Park hotel in Panama City, and that he would see me back there.

I climbed back down off the stage to rejoin my table and check that my case was still there. There were all kinds of drink sellers going around and one guy was selling some excellent posters of Roberto that I had never seen before of when he was in his prime. I asked the guy on our table with the deformity if he would go and get me one. He asked me for some dollars and I gave him a $10 dollar note. He came back with the poster (but no change) and I then bought him a soft drink. He then said he would get Roberto to sign it for me, and off he went. Roberto had changed into a Duran sports top by now and was mingling amongst the audience whilst the first boxing bout got underway.

Roberto was now sitting at ringside with his wife Fula and family and friends around him so I went over to meet them all.

My friend came back with the poster signed by Roberto and then Ismael Laguna took it from me and asked me to spell my name for him and he would also sign it; this he did. I then asked my friend if he would go and get another poster for me as I thought they would sell well back in the UK, but he returned to say that they were sold out of them.

I was really starting to feel the pace by now and getting tired, as I reckoned it must be about 5am UK time. There were only three bouts on and over three rounds and they appeared to be more like exhibition bouts as some were wearing headguards and others not. The Salsa bands were back up on stage and guess who had joined them? Yes it was Roberto. He sang along with the bands and was actually very good; he also played the bongos. The crowd were enjoying him and dancing in the aisles. This went on for about an hour until the close.

The big Jamaican guy told me that he would sort out my taxi back to the hotel. Outside the arena there were a lot of drunks about singing and shouting and something told me to be careful as I was hanging onto my suitcase tightly. The Jamaican pulled a cab over and I climbed into the back seat and he followed me in; this made me wonder what he was getting in for. His deformed friend also tried to get in but the bigger guy told him to go away. I then noticed he was still carrying my poster so I asked him to pass it to me but he pulled it back and asked me for some dollars. I was in no mood or place to start an argument so I passed him a few dollars and off we went.

My minder spoke to the cab driver in whatever language and asked me if I wanted to go to a club or to have some fun. I said no way, that I was tired as I had been travelling a long time and just wanted to get to bed. We pulled up outside the hotel and he asked the driver how much for me. It was only about $10 dollars which was not bad for the distance we appeared to have travelled. He carried my bag into the hotel for me and I went to reception and rang for service.

The beautiful Panamanian girl at reception asked my name and then said there was no room booked for a Mr Devlin; I then asked her if it had been booked as Mr Dublin as this had been the name that my flights were booked in. Once more she said there was no room for a Mr Dublin either. Then my brain stating ticking over and there was one last chance, so I asked if there was a room booked for Mr Buchanan? Oh yes! Mr Buchanan's suite is on the top floor. Thank you, I said and she gave me the room key. My big minder carried my case up for me and came into the immaculate room with me; this made me nervous. He stood there staring at me and then asked me what time tomorrow, I said about lunchtime. He still just stood there and I said goodnight. He said that he needed some dollars to get back home. I pulled out a $10 dollar note and he said that was not enough as he lived at the far side of Panama. I said to him that's all that I had and he still insisted on a few more dollars, and gave me such a grim stare, so I gave him a couple more and off he went. I hoped that would be the last I would see of him and thank God it was.

I took a look around the room, which was absolutely immaculate and the views were stunning across the sea. There was a letter addressed to Mr Buchanan welcoming him to Panama as their guest at the executive club. If only Ken knew what he was missing? I quickly unpacked my case best I could and fell onto the bed wondering what time it was. Here I was in Panama, and although I was very tired I did not want to sleep in case I missed anything for the short time that I was going to be here.

The next morning I woke, showered and got dressed, watched a little TV which had coverage of the Duran function on and then went down to the reception area to take a look around. As I passed the desk one of the girls on the desk called over to me: "Mr Bookanan". I headed towards her and thought she was going to ask me for some ID or something but all she wanted was my autograph. I was not going to start explaining that I wasn't Ken Buchanan again as there was still the chance that I might get thrown out of the hotel so once again I quickly signed for her in my best Scottish handwriting. The girl then told me that breakfast was now available in the executive suite near my room; I smiled and asked her what room Tony Gonzalez was in? She told me so I thanked her, and she mumbled something to her assistant but all I could make out was the name Bookanan.

After breakfast I went to my room and called Tony who eventually answered and said that he would see me downstairs later. I went down into the reception area where a small group of guys were sitting and all chatting about boxing. I looked over and noticed a few faces from the previous night's function. I went over to them and introduced myself, telling them why I was there and they did likewise. One of them was dressed in a shell suit and it was Ray Lampkin who had been up on stage the previous night dressed in a tuxedo and Stetson. Ray was one of Roberto's world title opponents, in fact the first to take him into the fourteenth round although he was knocked out cold in that round by Roberto's vicious left hook.

We all sat and chatted about our interests within the sport and the differences between the States and the UK. A guy called Chip and his pal Vern were forming an organisation that helped ex-boxers with certain needs within the state of Oregon, which was where Ray Lampkin was from. Ray spoke with a very slow drawl but was quite charming and down to earth. An elderly guy joined our company and I was informed that he was an ex-referee who had refereed a lot of Roberto's fights in Panama, mainly at the stadium where the tribute night had been held. He spoke very slow, broken English, but kept you held with his stories about the bouts. One of the group had brought along with him some video tapes of Roberto's fights and within the hotel complex were a few small shops.

One of the shops happened to be a TV and video shop so we went in asked one of the guys if there was a possibility that he might put the tape on for us. After explaining to him who we were and why we were there, he said no problem and put the tape in for us.

We all stood watching Roberto knocking over several of his early opponents and then the old referee was showing us himself on screen and explaining a little about how to referee fights properly without getting too involved and spoiling the contest – which some modern referees tend to do.

Then Ray Lampkin's fight against Roberto came on and there was not a great lot in the fight until the latter rounds when Roberto started to get through with some hard right hands and left hooks. One of the punches appeared to catch Ray full on the chin, and Chip turned round to Ray and said, "that must've hurt, Ray" to which Ray replied jokingly, "I never felt a thing". When the fight went into the fourteenth round Roberto caught Ray with a peach of a left hook and down he went for the full count of ten. At this point with the doctor in the ring, Ray once again jokingly said to us that he "never felt a thing". Luckily he recovered and was alright after the bout.

Oscar, who was Roberto's son in law, watched the video with us and I asked him what Roberto was like back home and where he lived. He said that he still lived in Panama but also stayed in Miami a lot. He said that he often went with him on Sundays when Roberto goes with some of his older friends down to a little place in Panama where they all fish and cook what they catch and then all play dominoes together in a small shack. Oscar also said that he had visited the area where Roberto was brought up and it was still pretty desperate, but Roberto still goes there and visits friends and gives hand-outs to the kids there and that he was a great family man.

We all watched a few more bouts until the tape ended and then I was approached by one of the hotel porters asking me if I would come and meet one of the guests who was requesting an autograph from Mr Bookanan. I went over and obliged and Chip and Vern had a good laugh about it as I had informed them as to what had happened at the airport when I arrived.

Tony Gonzalez then came into the lobby with Irichelle and Roberto's wife and other daughter. He asked if we were all ok and enjoying ourselves and informed us that we might be going to watch the Sugar Shane Mosley v Vernon Forest rematch at a pub on the big-screen tonight. Tony said that he was going to do some shopping and that he would see us all later.

Chip, Vern and I sat and listened to the old referee telling us tales about himself and Panama. I asked him his name so that I could inform those back home about him. He told me and then I asked if he would write it down for me. I gave him a pen and paper and he started off but then really struggled and he then told us all a story about how he had had some kind of accident with his hand and could not write very well. He eventually finished writing his name, which we could barely make out and he then amazingly stood up and took a business card from his pocket with his name on. He was, in fact, Isaac Herrera and had refereed Roberto's fight against Ray Lampkin. We all wondered why on earth he had not just produced the card in the first place.

Ray Lampkin said he fancied a walk, so I went with him and we went from the hotel for a stroll up the street and as it was really hot and humid I went into a small shop and bought a couple of bottles of coke. We stood outside the shop and then all of a sudden the heavens opened with rain. We took shelter under the shop canopy and a car pulled up alongside us and an untidily dressed guy got out carrying a tray with some kind of doughnuts and cookies on and asked if we would buy some from him. We both refused and he took off in his car. We had barely been standing there over a minute when another car pulled in and this time another guy got out of the car carrying a long cloth belt full of different sized and shaped knifes, asking how many dollars we would give him for all of them, and then tried to sell them separately. Once again we said no and off he went. I got the impression there were some desperate people living in that area who would try and sell anything for a few dollars.

Ray was a nice guy but said he did not have much work going for him back home in Oregon. We then went inside out of the rain back to the hotel where we met up with Chip and Vern. We all wandered into the back of the hotel grounds where we took a few photos and then went and had some snacks at the hotel dining room.

We arranged to meet up in reception at 7pm to meet Tony Gonzalez. Tony and Irichelle arrived on time and organised our transport to a bar called Hennigan's which was only about ten minutes' drive away. Tony was driving a luxurious white car which he said was Roberto's.

At the pub we went upstairs into a private room set up with the big-screen and there was a long table with the name ROBERTO DURAN written on a piece of card in felt tip.

We all took our seats. I sat next to Ray Lampkin and then Pipino Cuevas and his wife came in with Vinny Pazienza and his lady friend. We had waitress service all night with free drinks and food. Then the Mosley versus Forrest fight came on ...what more could you want?

Irichelle was asking everybody who would win. I honestly thought Mosley would win but Ray Lampkin said that Forrest had his number, and how right he was. After the fight we all left for the hotel. Chip and I were driven back by a wild character whose name I can't recall but as he was driving he was trying to show us the belt he had strapped around his waist. It was inscribed with 'the Latin world champion' and he said it was one of Roberto's. He told us the story about it, but we could not make head nor tail of him at all.

Chip and I went back into the hotel and straight to our rooms, as the jet lag was catching up on us and we were both tired.

After breakfast the next morning I checked my flight time which was around late afternoon. Chip and company had already left so I took a last look around the hotel and I bought a little gift for my daughter Joy and gave the lady a $10 dollar tip which she was ecstatic about and asked if I was sure that I did not want it back. Then one of the porters shouted over to me "Mr Bookanan". He came over to me and said a gentleman would like to meet me. The middle aged Latin American gentleman was with his wife and three daughters and came over to me and said in broken English that he was very pleased to meet me and that he had seen me box a few times at different venues. I shook his hand and gave his wife a kiss on the cheek and his daughters giggled with excitement. He asked me to sign for him on one of the Panamanian Sunday newspapers; I could do no other than oblige his request and signed Ken Buchanan once again in my best Scottish handwriting.

I packed my case and left the hotel. Outside there were any amount of cab drivers awaiting so one the hotel porters came over to me and asked for one of them to take Mr Bookanan to the airport. I got into the cab and the young driver first of all asked me what time my flight was and when I told him he said I was far too early. I asked him about Roberto and he said that he would drive me to Roberto's house as it was not that far away.

He pulled up outside the house which was in the middle of a normal town street and looked quite old with a few extensions added to it, very similar to the houses you would see in Spanish resorts. There were large double gates outside and a poster advertising his tribute night on the wall. There was an old motorbike standing in the yard with a seat near it and several empty bottles. The driver said Roberto would often sit there playing with his grandchildren. He said that he used to keep a young lion at home but it had died and he thought that he had a pet monkey now. He said Roberto was a kind man but a little crazy with his money, and that he loved to wine, dine, and have a good time. I hung around a while but there was obviously no one at home.

I asked the driver if we had time to have a look at the Panama Canal. He said it should be all right as long as we did not stay too long. Panama is only famous for two things as far as I am concerned and I had seen and met one in Roberto Duran, so I thought I may as well take a quick look at the other within the short time I had left.

The canal was a lot bigger than I expected and is a lake with series of docks at each end which fill up and lift the ships up to it and down again on the other side. As I looked at the canal I thought about my father who had died aged 72 on 14 January 1996 and had worked in shipyards most of his life. I bet a lot of the ships he had worked on would have passed through the canal; how I wished he had been here with me to see it.

I did not have a lot of time to hang around so the cab driver put his foot down and took me to the airport where I was soon on my way back to Newcastle via London and Miami.

When I arrived home it still took a while to sink in where I had been and everybody back home wanted to know what it had been like in Panama.

MARTYN OUTSIDE ROBERTO'S HOUSE, PANAMA, JULY 2002

ROBERTO'S HOUSE, PANAMA

MARTYN WITH ROBERTO DURAN'S MOTHER, PANAMA, 2002

MARTYN IN PANAMA WITH REFEREE ISAAC HERRERA

ROBERTO DURAN'S NAME ON PAVEMENT STAR, PANAMA

THE FIRST TOUR

I now had to start work with promoters who had heard about Roberto and were now hopefully interested in featuring him on a UK tour.

I had to stage six shows to get him over at a fee that would be acceptable to them so that they could make their own profits. Unlike me, most of these guys were in the game of promoting for a living and would not take anybody on that they could not make a profit out of, but I had the contact with Roberto and it was up to me to make it work this time as they had all been a bit doubtful about him coming over last time.

I always found that the best time to tour over here was either March or October time as the annual summer holidays were then over and it was not too close to Xmas so I decided along with Tony Gonzalez that we should go for early October. Tony said that Roberto was booked for the first week elsewhere so we went for the second week in October.

I contacted the interested promoters and had three definite shows with Glyn Rhodes, Dave Furnish, and Kevin Sanders who all staged similar shows annually. This meant that I still had to come up with three more to get Roberto at the agreed fee. I contacted the majority of other promoters in the UK but did not receive a reply from any of them. I then contacted John Celebanski from Bradford who appeared to be interested and had a call from Chris Sanigar from Bristol who was also interested.

I worked with the interested promoters and let them know how best to stage the shows so that they would get the most from Roberto and also how to get extra revenue from the photos I would supply them with.

I became a member of an agents' organisation which gave legal advice which was necessary for this type of tour involving international contracts but I also included some of my own ideas into the contracts. I worked to the same contract that we had done previously but had to issue contracts that were governed by UK law to the promoters over here, although my own contract was governed by US law. This was obviously a risk, which meant that if things went wrong I would be liable both in the US and the UK courts, so I had to get it right first time, and had to cover myself at every stage to both keep Roberto and Tony happy along with the promoters. I knew this was not going to be easy but thought what the hell! How many people would have the chance to spend a week travelling with a legend of Duran's calibre? Although it was always a gamble as you never knew what he would be like to travel around the country with for seven days, I was quite confident that he would be ok as we'd built up a friendship between us especially proven by him inviting me to Panama.

The problem now was the final show to complete the six required. I contacted an acquaintance from the amateur game in Liverpool and let him know about Roberto coming over and how he could make it happen as Roberto was not attending any shows in that area of the country.

I sent him some details about it and also the video tape of 'Beyond the glory' which was an excellent tape showing a few behind the scenes lifestyle of Roberto and was very good for promotional work. The guy was a former amateur boxer and also running a sandwich business so should know plenty of contacts to do a show.

It appeared that he was going to go for it and it was just a case of sorting a venue out, so I sent him the contract to sign and return back to me. Time was starting to run out now as deposits had to be sent over to the States as there was no way that Tony and Roberto were going to come all the way over here without a deposit. Tony was very firm on clauses within the contract and the timing of the deposit payment was always highlighted.

I received a call from the Liverpool guy to say that after reading the contract and finding out he had to send a deposit within a set time he had decided not to go ahead with it and was pulling out.

That's all I needed with only a few months to go and only five shows booked. I was left with no other option than to put the final show on myself. After struggling the first time round this was going to be hard so the only way I could do it was to keep the ticket price rock bottom and find a large local venue and hopefully cover the cost.

Roberto had already been to Newcastle so I decided to look somewhere closer to home and deal with local contacts. The only available place was the Temple Park Leisure Centre at South Shields which had a large hall that was used for indoor sports.

I went down to the centre, took a look around and decided to go for it. Time was not on my side and once the venue was booked I could start organising the MC, big-screen, entertainment and posters, programmes and all of the other promotional items that go with staging such an event – but most of all the ticket sales.

Staging events like this are a big task, but once you've done a few, things do fall into place, but it is by no way easy. I like to try and get things to perfection and you have to work hard to get this, because only you can do it as others who turn up to help out on the night won't give a monkey's about it so long as they have a good time, get paid and have their photographs or autograph with the celebrities.

At most functions the majority of those attending don't realise all the hard work that has to be done behind the scenes and quite a few come on the night and look for something to complain about. I always say to myself this is the last one I am doing and often wonder why I bother, but it is nice to get the chance to meet the champions of your chosen sport and gives you a buzz when it's all done and you can look back on the night and still talk about it for years later.

One of our regular attendee businessmen contacted me to book a table. He is one of those guys that will complain about anything he can think of. He will complain about seating arrangements (although you usually have to wait on his money), complain about the food, and having to queue for his photo, the comedian etc, etc, but in this game it is all down to ticket sales and you cannot refuse these whingers such as him as much as you would like to.

I only usually deal with a couple of the smaller businessmen and have never been one for chasing up the corporate side, but I have built up a fair size clientele over the years by just aiming at the genuine fight fans who have a similar interest in meeting the champions and listening to their stories from their careers.

So the six shows were now booked, the deposits paid and sent over to Tony. I now had to target individuals to try and sell tables of ten to pay for the show. This might sound easy... but is it hell? The majority will agree to it on the night in the pub, but once it comes down to getting the money from them it is a different story. Obviously the hard part was that the majority of those up here in Newcastle had already seen Roberto, so why go to see him again? So I had to target different local areas and keep the ticket price as low as possible.

The show was booked for a Friday night which meant that it was a good night for anybody wanting to travel up and stay over but a bad night for quite a few of our regulars who worked as pub doormen. South Shields is a small seaside town full of pubs and night-clubs and guesthouses so I had to use this to help with those travelling from out of the area as a selling point.

I was then hit with a further obstacle when the Leisure Centre, which is council run, hit me with a bill for £600 for the room hire charge for the function. It's amazing that you can bring a legend like Roberto Duran to a leisure centre in a small town like this which helps to put it on the map, giving it publicity, not forgetting the small fortune that they could make in bar takings and sales of bar snacks and they still want more from you. This annoyed me so I contacted a local councillor for the area and explained my concern to him.

The councillor acknowledged receipt of my request and said he would contact the head of leisure services. The head replied saying that at £20 a head someone must be going to make a lot of money out of it. I think he was under the impression that Roberto was coming over free of charge along with his lawyer and daughter and that they were getting free flights from Panama and their hotel was paid for and I just had to pay for the evening's MC entertainment, big-screen hire, tickets, programmes, posters, door staff, raffle staff, etc, etc. He did, however, give a little bit of leeway though by stating that if the bar takings were good he would reduce the hall hire charge.

It was a pity none of the local workingmen's clubs in the area where large enough as they would have jumped at the chance. But this was the typical of the local council not recognising the fact that I was bringing a legend to them and the opportunity was there for them to cash in on it.

Time went by and all the shows were now confirmed. Tony contacted me to let me know that instead of bringing Roberto's son with him it would be Roberto's daughter Irichelle, whom I had met in Panama. He also informed me of their flight arrival times in London. I did try to get them to fly up to Leeds Bradford airport where the first show was being held, but he was having none of it and said that he expected all internal travel to be met by the promoters.

I had decided to insert into the contract a clause that whoever had Roberto on a set night would have to pick him up from the previous night's venue. The reason for this being that in the first case we would not have a problem driving around cities looking for hotels or venues, and it would not be costing me for transport and on the road snacks etc; along with this it would give us the chance to meet the other promoters and his team before the event. I did check out the flight price from London to Leeds and it was very reasonable so I informed John Celebanski the promoter at Bradford of this and he did agree that after a ten hour flight from Miami, the last thing they would want is to be stuck in a car for four hours travelling up from London.

I left Newcastle airport for Heathrow on the 6.30am flight and then went across to terminal three to await their arrival, which was due in at 10.40 am.

I waited at the arrival point and kept a check on the monitor which said that the flight was due on time, so I went and had a coffee. It then came over the monitor that their flight had landed but so had another two flights around the same time.

Hundreds of passengers came through the arrivals gate but I could see no sign of Roberto or Tony. I asked a guy coming through what flight he had been on and he said the Miami flight. There was then a pause when no one was coming through. I started to sweat and wonder, as this time I had been quite certain they would arrive and was never in any real doubt. Then after a pause another crowd started coming through that were off another American Airlines flight. I was really starting to panic now: how the hell would I explain to the other promoters that he had not turned up?

I then heard a lot of fast Spanish chat going on amongst the next crowd coming through and then I spotted him, dressed in a black roll neck jumper, black slacks and a black New York baseball hat, the legend himself... Roberto Duran, with Tony Gonzalez and Roberto's daughter Irichelle alongside him.

I waved them over and they greeted me with their usual handshake and a hug. They all looked very tired and in need of a rest. I took them over to the coffee lounge and checked out the time of our connecting flight to Leeds, which was not due to leave for another two hours yet. Tony asked if I could get us on an earlier flight. I said I would go and try, but on asking there was no earlier flight so we were going to have to wait.

I ordered some coffees and we sat around till our call came. No one had recognised Roberto; although a legend in boxing he was just another person passing through the airport. Irichelle spoke quite good English but appeared to be very tired. We went up into the waiting lounge and found a seating area. I bought Irichelle a magazine, and Roberto got stretched out on the padded seating area and pulled his baseball cap over his eyes, whilst Tony went for a walk.

When we boarded the plane there were plenty of spare seats and Roberto sat opposite me and went straight back to sleep. I noticed he was wearing what appeared to be a pair of blue clog-like shoes. As we were preparing to land the air hostess had to wake him up to lower his armrest and fasten his seatbelt; he said thank you. I noticed that Roberto constantly took off his cap and ran his fingers through his immaculate, thick, jet-black hair.

On arrival at Leeds we were met by an elderly chap and taken to a white limousine, and then on to the Holiday Inn hotel. At the Hotel the promoter John Celebanski and his assistant John Walsh met us. John Celebanski, a former decent professional heavyweight, was quite laid back and showed us to our rooms, as he knew Roberto and his party would need some sleep. I asked John if I could take a look at the function room so he took me down and told me how he ran his shows and asked if I had the entrance theme tape. I gave the tape to John and when he tried to play it on the system no sound came out. He contacted reception for the guy who handled that arrangement but apparently the guy was away and someone else had been left to sort it out but he did not know how to, so that was the entrance music plan done away with.

John told me to bring Roberto down to the lounge area at a set time, so that the important sponsors could meet him first and then he could eat in private and then be introduced to the function hall audience later. This was to help with the four hour appearance which was in the contract. Roberto met the main sponsors in the private lounge and was great with them acknowledging for photos and autographs. Irichelle was a little taken back because this show was a black tie event and she said that she had only brought her denims and casual clothes with her and felt under-dressed for the show, but I told her not to worry and that she still looked great anyway.

Whilst Roberto, Tony and Irichelle ate privately, I went in to the hall and sat on the top table and had the meal that took over two and a half hours to serve. Then they brought Roberto in to a huge ovation. The MC then went on for over 30 minutes introducing the top table and also trying to do a comedy spot in between. A comedian followed him who was not much better. They then asked Roberto questions from the audience to which he answered perfectly well, with Tony interpreting for him.

After this John asked me to take Roberto to each table but I thought this might be a little unsafe, as quite a few of the guests were now well served with drink as the night had taken so long so I suggested to the two security lads to set a table up at the end of the room and let them queue for photos and autographs. They agreed with me and that's the way it worked although one of the security lads disappeared as did some of the committee and I had to end up helping with organising the queue and those who were coming back for more autographs. Roberto stayed until they were all happy and then we all retired to our rooms.

The next morning I met up with John Celebanski and he was more than pleased with Roberto and Tony, and then we had a coffee together and waited for Roberto to come down to breakfast. Time was getting on but then Roberto, Tony and Irichelle all came down together and ordered breakfast.

John Walsh, the chairman, came in with a huge bag of boxing gloves and photos that Roberto kindly signed for him and he asked Roberto to pose for more photos. John Celebanski was no problem and more than happy with just one photo with Roberto. John Walsh brought out a huge photo album of his with shots of him with several celebrity stars and one of him with Roberto at a Las Vegas show.

At breakfast Roberto was amazed by a brass coffee decanter on the table and asked the waitress how it worked. The lady showed him and I thanked her; she then later asked me if he would like one. To my amazement she brought one from her cupboard and gave it to him, for which he was very grateful.

We all chatted for a while and then Chris Sanigar, who was the promoter at the next show at Bristol, rang me for directions to the hotel, as his driver had arrived in Bradford. He then told me that the driver was none other than Glenn Catley who was the former 2000 World super middleweight champion. I passed the phone to one of the staff who directed Glenn to the hotel, and I greeted him when he arrived along with his friend. Roberto had never heard of him but greeted him as he did with everybody.

The vehicle was a people carrier, which was quite small when we were all jammed in with our entire luggage. Roberto took the front passenger seat and off we set for Bristol, which was a three hour journey.

Roberto opened a small blue rucksack and pulled out some cassette tapes and asked Glenn if he could put them on for him. Then the fun started. The tapes were the same Salsa music that I had heard back in Panama and Roberto started off with his singing. He sang them word for word, made dance actions with his hands and every now and again would scream out loud and then laugh, after which we all followed suit and he had us all laughing. Glenn was in his element and said to me that it was an honour to be driving Roberto Duran but to be serenaded by him was something else. We stopped for a coffee on the way and Roberto sat with us while Tony and Irichelle did some shopping. Roberto was very humorous and talked constantly although he spoke little English; he had his own way of making you understand and certainly made you laugh.

When we were back on the road I received a call from a guy asking where Roberto was on that night. He then called back to ask where he would be the rest of the week. Unbelievably he said that all he wanted was some gloves signed by Roberto and even asked our whereabouts on the motorway so he could come and meet Roberto and get them signed. Some people will do anything but pay for a ticket. I told him he would have to attend one of the shows to meet Roberto, but that he was not signing gloves anyway. He was probably just another memorabilia dealer.

Irichelle was obviously feeling tired and uncomfortable with the long journey and kept asking how long it was going to be before we arrived at Bristol. I kept telling her we were nearly there even though I knew we were still an hour away.

On arriving at Bristol Roberto started his antics by winding down the window and shouting BRISTOL, BRISTOL, DURAN HERE! He had us all, plus passing motorists, in fits of laughter. We met up with the Promoter Chris Sanigar who was typically stressed out with organising everything and said he would have to rush and change from his track-suit as he had a press photographer awaiting a photo of Roberto with Chris. We went to our rooms at the immaculate Jury's hotel in the centre of Bristol and I then went downstairs to take a look at the function room. I was introduced to the MC who was none other than John McDonald who often works on the TV big fights. John was professional and wanted everything to be on time with no hiccups.

I did let Chris know that Roberto must be paid his fee before he made his appearance; he said that this was ok but wanted Roberto to sign some items first and then he would pay him; he even took me to his room and showed me the dollars. I called Tony Gonzalez and informed him of this, but he said that this was no good and that Roberto must be paid before he makes his appearance. I tried to contact Chris but was told he was in the function room as the dinner was now being served. Chris was at the top table so I went up to him and let him know what Tony had said. I feared a problem as Chris seemed very thorough in doing things his way but he very calmly pulled the payment out of his inside pocket and passed the notes to me.

I called Roberto at his room to let him know about the time that they wanted us down for signings and he asked me if I could get him something to eat as he was hungry. Luckily there was a waitress who spoke fluent Spanish so I passed the phone to her and it was sorted.

I met up with Tony at my room as we did at each show and I counted out the payment for him on the bed. We then called Roberto and went to a private room outside the function room and met Chris. Chris then pulled out several pairs of gloves and framed pictures that he wanted Roberto to sign for him and he already had an impressive glass glove case made up that his son Jamie had stuck the signed gloves in alongside a signed photo which looked great for auctioning. Roberto spent about ten minutes signing the items and then Chris pulled out about another 100 photos for him to sign. Roberto said something to Tony, but got started on them; however, he only got so many signed before it was time for us to go into the function room.

John McDonald gave his usual grand entrance introduction to Roberto, and a mention to Tony and Irichelle but none to me and I also had to find my own seat behind the top table guests.

This did cheese me off a little to think that it was me who had done all the hard work to bring Roberto over.

The question and answer session was similar to Bradford, but the guests were squeezed into the room like sardines, and John McDonald had a bit of a job on getting to them with the microphone. The photo session at the end was a little disorganised as Roberto was just left to stand on his own until someone eventually decided to get a table over for him to sit at, although he did not sign any autographs there as Chris did not allow this and said if they wanted an autograph they would have to buy one of his photos that Roberto had previously signed. The security on the night was down to one man and that was Chris Sanigar. What Chris Sanigar says goes at Bristol, and he appeared to control everything himself.

The next morning after breakfast I received a call from Glyn Rhodes, the next show promoter at Sheffield. Glyn said that he was well on his way from Sheffield and enquired about directions to the hotel. I informed him we were bang in the centre of Bristol alongside the river and next to a large car park. He wondered if they would be allowed to park their limousine outside the hotel. I enquired about this and the staff said that it should not be a problem.

Glyn and his team of four arrived around late morning, as I was sitting chatting to Chris and Jamie. Glyn was a real down to earth guy, and was amazed when I showed him a programme from my amateur days when he and I had boxed on the same bill at Sheffield during 1978.

Roberto eventually surfaced, came down with Tony and Irichelle and as usual asked for something to eat. I did the introductions to Glyn and his team and we then got our bags together and set off for Sheffield.

Unbeknown to me Glyn had brought a young reporter by the name of Mark along with him who started to fire questions at Roberto and Tony as we travelled. I noticed Mark was taking down shorthand and also had a tape recorder and microphone lying on the floor of the limousine. I sat next to Roberto in the back of the limousine and he appeared to be OK with the questions but then became agitated when asked about the relations between the USA and Panama. We pulled into a service station and the limousine driver who was an Asian guy named Ray showed Roberto one of the new smart mobile phones which had a photo of a seductive blonde on its screen. Roberto was amazed by this and asked if he could have one; Ray said he would see what he could do for him once they arrived in Sheffield. Once back in the limousine, Roberto said he was tired and did not want to answer any more questions so he then put his headphones on and his salsa music tapes and once again sang along with them. The limousine was a top of the range one and was fitted with the laser graphics of the CD player; Roberto was quite amused by this. The journey took around three hours, which was quite good for such a huge car.

As we approached Sheffield Glyn asked me if Roberto would call into his boxing gym to see the youngsters who were too young to attend the show before we went to the hotel. I said it should not be a problem as we were in good time and it was on the way.

As we approached the gym Glyn informed me that his gym was based in an old school that had been used for the filming of the Full Monty, an award winning film about a group of working class Sheffield fellows who strip off to raise cash.

The gym was a typical one, quite small but with lots of punch bags and a small ring to one side. A group of young amateur boxers were standing waiting to see Roberto; the majority of them were probably too young to realise what an honour this was having a legend such as Roberto visit their gym, but there were also a few senior boxers there.

As he walked into the gym you could sense Roberto felt at home. He went straight over and threw a couple of punches at the bags and then swung one of the small maize balls and from a standing position slipped his head from side to side as it swung an inch or so past his face. He made this look so easy and the kids seemed fascinated by it.

Roberto then climbed into the ring for a local photographer and posed for a few shots. However the photographer was taking too long and asking for more shots to which Roberto replied am I getting paid for this? This was Roberto's way of letting him know that he had enough. Roberto then invited one of the youngsters into the ring with him and showed him how to turn his opponent in a corner, by taking punches on the arms and then turning him bodily so that he then had his opponent cornered. He then invited one of the senior boxers into the ring and showed him the same move. The kids loved this and applauded Roberto as we left.

We all climbed back into Ray's limousine and as we drove off I noticed that young Mark, the reporter, had been left behind, Glyn laughed and said he would catch up with us later.

We stayed at the Hilton hotel in Sheffield which was a surprise as Glyn had informed me that we would be staying at the Grosvenor Hotel where the show was being held, but he decided to change things for his own reasons.

At the function Steve Holdsworth gave us an excellent introduction and the audience of around 400 gave Roberto a fantastic reception. I sat next to Irichelle and the night's comedian who was a real funny guy that had some great banter with the audience. Former heavyweight contender Earnie Shavers also attended the show and sat on the top table alongside us.

Roberto was his usual self with the question and answer session and had the audience in the palm of his hand. I had mentioned to Glyn Rhodes previously that Roberto was quite good at playing the bongo drums, and somehow out of the blue Glyn acquired a pair of bongo drums and brought them up to the top table to Roberto.

Roberto was laughing about this but then put the drums between his knees and started to rattle a tune out. One of the organisers brought a microphone right up to the drums so that all of the audience could hear this. The drum beat that Roberto played for a minute or so had a proper rhythm to it and all of the audience started to clap along with it – it was absolutely brilliant.

We were then were taken to a private room where the photos were going to be taken. I noticed the photographer was none other than Paul Speak, the guy who had driven Ricky Hatton to the Newcastle show and was now working as his agent. The session was disorganised at first as most shows were, but then Glyn got things moving and a pattern developed of one group in at a time as the others left. Glyn was very strict and only allowed the merchandise that he was selling on the night to be autographed and nothing else which appeared to upset quite a few customers, but does help to stop the memorabilia merchants from using your efforts to line their own pockets. One of those who were refused their photograph with Roberto was Mark the young reporter who had travelled with us but for some reason Glyn would not let him near Roberto.

Glyn had a few pals in the function that owned some kind of bar restaurant and asked us if we would like to go back there for a few drinks. These guys were of mixed race and very smart and friendly towards us all. Within the bar restaurant there were a few pictures on the wall of Che Guevara and Fidel Castro. Tony and Roberto were discussing them in Spanish and I recall Roberto going up and putting a serviette over the picture of one of them.

We all sat around for a while chatting then Roberto asked for some food. Glyn's friends said they would order it for us but we sat waiting for half an hour and nothing came. Glyn then got on the phone to his beautiful wife and asked her to sort the food and bring it to the hotel where we were staying.

So off we went in the limousine and back to the hotel. I thought we may have a problem bringing the food in but we were told to go to the upstairs bar which was still open for wine. When Glyn's wife arrived with the food we were all like scavengers and it went in no time.

I sat chatting with Glyn and his wife. Irichelle decided to go to her room, but Roberto and Tony sat chatting with the Pakistani restaurant owner guy and Ray the Asian limousine driver. They started telling Roberto and Tony tales of their lives back in their homelands and Tony was in absolute stitches of laughter. I had never heard him laugh so much; the Pakistani guy had him absolutely rolling on the couch with laughter with whatever tales he was telling them about. After a couple of hours of entertaining chat, we all decided to retire to our rooms.

The next morning we all had a bit of a lie in, and I went for breakfast about 10am, but there was no sign of Roberto or Tony.

I received a call from John Walsh, the guy who I'd sat next to at the Bradford show and who had brought all of the gloves to be signed the following morning. He said that he had driven over from Bradford to bring some of the caricature pictures of Roberto over for him because he liked them. I said it was very kind of him, and he said he would meet me in reception. I went down to reception but there was no sign of him, so I went back to my room. I then received a call from John asking where I was; I immediately went down to reception but once again there was no John Walsh.

Then the penny dropped: I had forgotten to tell John that Glyn Rhodes had changed the hotel where we were staying for his own security reasons, so I was waiting to meet John in the reception at the Hilton and he was over at the Grosvenor Hotel where the function had been held and where we were originally staying overnight. I therefore let John know where we were staying now and said I would wait on him in reception. This time he was there but when I met him I noticed he had brought yet another bag full of gloves to sign in exchange for the pictures. I said I would have to ask Tony about this first, as I did think it was a bit cheeky especially after already having several gloves signed by Roberto at Bradford.

I went upstairs and met Tony and Roberto in the breakfast room. I informed Tony about John downstairs and he said that Roberto already had enough pictures and he had also signed enough gloves for John, so I went back downstairs and gave John the bad news. John was not happy about this as he had travelled all the way from Bradford to bring these pictures for Roberto, and asked me once again if he gave me some of the pictures would Roberto sign just a couple of pairs of gloves for him. I said I would ask him when he came down but to try and smooth things over for him I said I would give him his petrol money and I would take half of the pictures from him. He agreed to that but still hung around awaiting Roberto coming downstairs.

By this time Glyn Rhodes had turned up with his two youngsters who had told a white lie and taken the day off school. I had a bit of a laugh with them and we all said our farewells at the breakfast table as I was informed that our driver for the next show at Peterborough had turned up.

I went downstairs to meet the driver who was in an average size people carrier, and put Irichelle's luggage and mine in the back. Roberto and Tony came down with their luggage and squeezed it in as best they could. John Walsh then appeared from nowhere with another pair of gloves and asked Roberto to sign them; Roberto being Roberto kindly obliged.

The next stop, Peterborough, was about a two-hour drive. Roberto asked the driver to put his salsa tape on as he was having trouble with the headphones on his walkman, so he then started singing his head off. Tony and Irichelle were very tired from the previous night and covered their heads over with coats and tried to sleep, but probably couldn't because of Roberto's singing. Kevin Sanders was the promoter at Peterborough. Kevin appeared to be very professional in the build up to his event and ran his own gym as a professional trainer and promoter, having trained Nigel Benn and Matt Skelton.

Skelton was a former Marshall Arts heavyweight who had fought in K9 and when he came on the pro boxing scene there were not many trainers keen to put their reputation on the line. Yet Kevin Sanders stepped forward and within two years Matt Skelton was British and Commonwealth champion. Kevin also took on the job of training Nigel Benn for his biggest fight with American Gerald McClellan at late notice after the champion split with Jimmy Tibbs. It appeared a no win situation for both under the circumstances, for Benn changing trainers at the last moment and Sanders ready to take the blame as a fall guy if things went wrong. Though tragically spoilt by the injuries sustained by Gerald, both Benn and Sanders triumphed in the face of adversity.

We arrived at Peterborough around mid afternoon and I introduced everybody to Kevin. We were bang in the middle of the town and booked into a hotel called the Bull which was also where the function was going to be held. The hotel was really old and busy being refurbished. We took our luggage out of the cab and the cab driver helped us out with the rest. At each show Roberto had been presented with some kind of gift and these all added to the luggage we had to carry and I usually ended up carrying a couple of these items for Roberto, such as framed pictures etc.

As this hotel was very old there were no lifts available so we had to carry everything up three flights of stairs. We all helped each other as there was no help from the hotel staff. Tony, Irichelle and I were on the same floor but Roberto was on the floor below us in a suite. Once in my room I noticed that my black leather briefcase, in which I had all of the contracts, cash and personal items such as photos from the previous shows, was missing. I went over to Irichelle's room and she told me that my bag was in Roberto's room. I went down to Roberto's room but could not get an answer so went back to my own room and rang his room number but once again there was no answer. I went down to reception and asked the girl on the desk if she had seen him but she said no and rang his room for me – but without reply. I took a stroll into the shopping centre right next to the hotel to see if he had gone for a stroll with Tony and Irichelle as they sometimes did to buy toiletries or gifts for back home, but there was no sign of them.

I then went back to the hotel and bumped into Kevin Sanders who took me through to the function room and showed me the set up. Kevin introduced me to Mike Goodall, the evening's MC, who was busy setting the PA system up along with the big screen etc. I gave Mike the entrance fanfare tape that he said he would use.

On the way back to my room the girl on reception said that she had seen Mr Duran come back into the hotel, so I went straight to his room which had large double doors and gave him a knock. Roberto was very careful about opening his door and would not open it unless he was sure who was there, but he knew my voice by now and when I told him about the bag he invited me in and there it was on the floor alongside his large case.

I then went back to reception where I met Kevin Sanders and asked him if he knew of anywhere where I could buy some headphones for Roberto's walkman because he was complaining that only one side was working. Kevin and I went over to one of the local electrical shops and Kevin bought a pair of headphones for Roberto. I had already taken a look at Roberto's walkman and I was sure these would be suitable.

We returned to the hotel and I gave Roberto a knock, gave him the headphones and said I would see him later. Back up at my room I had just taken a shower when I received a call from Irichelle. She asked if Roberto's small blue rucksack had been put in my room. I took a look around and said it was not there and asked what the problem was. Tony said Roberto thought there was a ghost in his room as one minute his blue rucksack was there and then after taking a shower it had disappeared. Tony and Irichelle then came up to my room and asked about the rucksack. I went down to Roberto's room with them and looked around for it but it was nowhere to be seen.

Roberto always carried this small blue rucksack with him as it contained his passport and the small personal gifts that he had been given on the tour, and also his own personal walkman system with his salsa tapes and headphones. He said to Tony that it was in his room and then he had taken a nap; when he woke up and discovered it had disappeared, he mentioned to Tony that there was a ghost in his room. We checked each of our rooms just in case it had been misplaced but without success.

I went to reception and reported it to the girl on the desk, who informed me that she had gone into his room for an autograph and photo, but obviously before he took his nap. She said that she would check with the porters and ask if it had been put in the lost luggage room.

It was getting close to show time now so I took a shower but also rang reception to ask if they had found anything yet to which they replied no, but would call me if the bag turned up. I rang Kevin Sanders and explained to him what had happened and also asked if he would bring the payment up to my room.

Kevin turned up with the payment and was already dressed for the show. The payment was still intact in a Bank seal but the amount written on the envelope was far short of the requested fee. I immediately pointed this out to Kevin who, after I showed him the contract, agreed with me and gave his wife Vivienne a call. Vivienne said there could not have been a mistake and she had got the requested amount from the bank. Kevin and I checked the amount written on the envelope against the contracted amount and it was nowhere near. This was all I needed now at a crucial time, especially with Roberto being upset about his bag having gone missing.

Kevin agreed with me that the amount was wrong and made a few phone calls and said he would have the correct amount as soon as possible. I phoned Tony up to let him know what had happened and he appeared to be fine about it but asked if there was any news on Robert's bag yet as it contained his passport and his presents from the previous shows along with his salsa music tapes. Once again I called reception but nothing had shown up yet.

I opened the envelope with the payment inside and started counting the notes out on the bed. After double checking the amount three times it was only a few dollars short. I couldn't believe it – the amount that was written on the envelope was nowhere near the amount inside the sealed packet. I immediately rang Kevin Sanders who was already on his way to my room. When I informed Kevin about the mistake, he said that I was an honest man and he would put the amount right within the hour.

I asked Tony to come to my room for the payment and explained what had happened. I asked him about Roberto and his lost bag, and said how it was a mystery how it had disappeared; he said they also found it strange but hoped it would turn up as otherwise we might have to go to the nearest Panamanian Embassy, which was in London, tomorrow, so that Roberto could be given clearance to be allowed to leave the country on the following Monday.

Anyway we had to get through tonight first so we went down to Roberto's room where he was still in his bathrobe and nowhere near ready. Tony spoke to him and then told me that Roberto insisted he was not going to make his appearance until his bag was found. Kevin Sanders then came along the passageway with a few pairs of gloves to be autographed and about 40 photos to be signed. I said that I would pass them on to Roberto but he was not happy about his missing bag; nevertheless I would do my best to get them signed. I passed them on to Tony and waited in the passageway.

After about 20 minutes Tony emerged and said Roberto would not be long now and had signed most of the photos. I passed the word onto Kevin who informed me that the audience were ready for us now. I quickly informed Tony and Irichelle who had also turned up and surprisingly they all came out of the room together.

Tony, Irichelle and I went up onto the top table first and then Mike Goodall gave Roberto his introduction to which he received a rapturous standing ovation. I sat next to Irichelle and on the other side of me was Duke McKenzie, the former three times world champion. Alongside Roberto sat Dave Boy Green and Charlie Magri, with whom I chatted as the night went on – along with Duke they came across as perfect gentlemen. The function room was packed and we were squashed like sardines on the top table. Irichelle said to me during the meal that we would have to take our turns eating to allow us elbow room, so we jokingly said ok now it's your turn to each other from time to time. In the audience near the front Duke was busy having a conversation with respected trainer Jim McDonnell who had the boxer Takaloo sitting alongside him. The room was certainly full of champions. The evening's comedian came over to me and said that he would do his spot before Roberto did the question and answer session but would Irichelle and Roberto be offended if he took his clothes off. I asked if he was kidding, to which he said no, but he would wear a huge false rubber penis over his own. I said it should be fine, but try not to offend us at the top table! He assured me that it would be ok. As it happened he was quite good and funny and stood with his back to us for a 20 minute spot. Roberto found him hilarious.

The question and answer session went ok with the same old questions and then we went down to the lounge area for photographs.

I walked into the lounge with Roberto and we stood in a corner of the room with no table or chair and then a small, disorganised crowd gathered around us. Roberto signed a few autographs but had nothing to rest on and then eventually a young photographer came over and tried unsuccessfully to organise a queue. I eventually went over to Vivienne Sanders and asked if she could try and get something better organised as things were getting out of hand and poor Roberto was standing waiting. I noticed Kevin Sanders had moved over to the other part of the lounge where there appeared to be a sing-song going on, and the next thing was that he took the microphone and started singing an Elvis song.

The photographer was only a young lad and did not appear to have any assistant with him or any idea of how to organise things. I tried to help him with getting a queue formed and someone to take details and this worked for a while but amazingly he then ran out of film, so there were quite a few disappointed fans left standing, with a legendary world champion in front of them and no one to take their photo alongside him.

Kevin Sanders asked us if we would go to a small bar with him where no one would bother us and we could all have a quiet drink together. We agreed to this and followed Kevin to the bar which was just within walking distance from the Bull hotel. We settled into a small area of the bar, which was apparently owned by a friend of Kevin's, and drinks were brought over for us. One guy who came over to meet Roberto was a bit of a trickster and he showed Roberto a trick with some coins that amazed Roberto so much that he asked him to show him how it was done; then Roberto started to perform it on him himself. He then showed Roberto a table game with matchsticks and the two of them played this for about half an hour to the point where Roberto was getting the better of him. At the bar I discussed the lost bag situation with Tony, as if the bag did not show up with Roberto's passport in, it meant we would have to leave Peterborough for London the following morning and go to the Panamanian embassy to try and sort things out. This was going to be a nightmare as I already booked and paid for our train tickets from Peterborough to Newcastle on the 1pm train and they were non-refundable.

Kevin then rounded us all up and said he would like to take us to another club, which again was within walking distance. This time the club was a night-club with a bar area which was where we headed. The bar was mainly full of youngsters so Roberto went unnoticed. We stayed here for a short while and then I decided to head back to the hotel and enquire about Roberto's bag. There was only a night porter on duty who had heard about the missing bag but said nothing had yet turned up and he gave me a sheet to fill in so that everything was recorded.

The next morning I went down to reception and once again enquired about the bag; none of the staff at the hotel appeared concerned and passed the buck from one to the other, so I asked to see the manager. A young guy turned up saying he was standing in for the manager and asked what the problem was. I did not lose my cool but let him know that his hotel was poor and that most of the staff were totally unhelpful and that I wished to inform the police of the missing bag. He said that was not a problem and told me to go ahead and do this.

There were no signs of Tony, Roberto, Irichelle or Kevin, so I decided to give Tony a ring and he said he would be down for breakfast soon. I sat near a guy at the breakfast table who appeared to be a professional businessman and he must have overheard me talking to the manger and he asked what the problem was. He said he was on business in Peterborough and could not believe it when I said that Roberto Duran was here staying at the hotel. He happened to tell me that he worked for the Ministry of Defence and would try and make a few enquiries for me as to where we would have to go to get a passport for Roberto. It just so happened then that Roberto came down alone and sat near us and ordered breakfast.

The guy could not believe it when he saw Roberto but immediately got on his mobile phone and got me the numbers of the Panamanian Embassy in London and the Passport office. He then finished his breakfast and asked if he could shake Roberto's hand.

I went to the reception desk and got the number of Peterborough police station and informed them of what had happened. The crime lady I spoke to was called Carol Barnes who gave me a crime number and started asking for a few personal details regarding Roberto which I could not provide. Luckily just then Tony appeared and I called him over to the phone to help answer her questions.

We decided that we must head for London as soon as possible as we were getting nowhere fast here, so got our entire luggage together, this time making sure we had every bag and suitcase. As we came downstairs Kevin Sanders appeared and asked if the bag had turned up. He said he would check with the people carrier who had brought us down from Sheffield but I had already done this. I thanked Kevin anyway and asked him to order us a cab as a matter of urgency as we were going to have a busy schedule, by having to travel to London and then back up to Newcastle to attend my own show at South Shields.

The cab came and it was only a ten minute drive to the rail station where I purchased our four tickets to London which was apparently only an hour's journey. The train was one of the older types with not many passengers on so we took a seat each. We arrived at King's Cross at about midday and decided to leave all of our large cases at the luggage department there and just carried our hand luggage with us, as it was £5 per item to leave in the station, so I also had to carry Roberto's framed pictures and prints that he had been presented with.

Within the station there was a black cab queue which we joined and waited only minutes before taking one and asking to be driven to Mayfair to the Panamanian Embassy. In the cab I placed my black leather briefcase on the floor in front of me to allow Roberto to sit next to me and Tony and Irichelle then climbed in. I folded the seat down in front of me and placed the framed pictures and pile of prints that I had purchased from John Walsh in Sheffield on top of it. The journey was only a short one but took about 20 minutes due to the traffic and traffic lights. The driver pulled up in the middle of the street outside the embassy and kept his engine running. Tony, Irichelle and Roberto jumped out, and I asked the driver how much the fare was. I picked up the framed picture and the large envelope full of prints off the top of the seat in front of me and climbed out of the cab and paid him. As he drove away I then realised I had left my leather briefcase under the front seat. I shouted to Tony who was knocking on the Embassy doors. I pulled in another cab and informed him as to what had happened; he gave me a phone number but said that it should be handed to the lost property office but because it was Friday it may take a week before it reached there and that was only if it was handed in, because with it being under the front seat the driver may not even see it and the next passenger could pick it up.

I went over to Tony to let him know what the driver had said, but said I would go back to King's Cross and maybe see the driver as that may be his run, and meet them back at the luggage department. I asked Tony if he would lend me the money to pay for our train fare back up to Newcastle – all of my money was in the case along with flight tickets from Newcastle to Bristol for the next show, tickets from Cardiff to London for the Sunday, along with about £300 in cash, debit card, passport, contracts, photo films and many other personal items that I would probably never see again, although I was hoping there was that slight chance.

I explained to the cab driver who took me back over to King's Cross what had happened and he advised me to cancel my debit cards immediately and inform the police and lost property office about my loss, but he said there were now so many cab drivers in London and he doubted if I would ever see my bag again.

At King's Cross I cancelled my cards and informed the local police and then went over to the cab queue hoping that I might recognise the driver who had taken us across to the Embassy. I strolled up and down a few times but knew I was wasting my time and imagined someone to be in a bar now having a good drink with my money.

I went across to the luggage department and waited on Tony, Roberto and Irichelle, hoping that they had some good news about his passport. When they returned Tony informed me that Roberto must go back to the passport office again on Sunday and they would issue a temporary passport which would allow Roberto to return home to Panama. That was good news as we were due back in London on the Sunday, but I told him that I had no luck with my lost briefcase and he gave me the dollars that I needed to buy our train tickets back up to Newcastle.

I had a bit of a run around as I had to stand in a queue to find out what time the next train was and then go to the exchange bureau to change Tony's dollars to sterling and then back again for our tickets, so we just missed one train and had to wait an hour for the next one which was at 3pm and would get us into Newcastle at 6pm, not giving us a lot of spare time as the show was due to start at 7.30pm.

Tony and Irichelle went over to one of the burger kiosks at the station and bought food for the four of us to eat whilst we awaited the train. The station was packed with people and we had sit on our cases to eat our food as there were no seating areas available, and we wanted to be near the front of the queue, although no one could tell us what platform the train would leave from until it arrived at the station.

When the train finally arrived it was mayhem trying to get on it with all of our cases and the glass framed pictures etc that I was carrying. We all got on but there was no way we could get seats together. Roberto sat about ten rows in front of me and Tony and Irichelle managed to get two seats together several rows behind me.

I noticed a big fat guy sat next to Roberto who made him look as though he was being pushed into the window. After about half an hour I noticed Roberto standing up and getting out of his seat; he started walking towards me and when I called him over and asked if everything was all right he looked at where he had been sitting and held his nose between his fingers and said "he stinks". I could not help but laugh at him as he waddled back up the train to find another seat.

We arrived at Newcastle at about 5.45pm and I dashed to the compartment where we had left our luggage and dragged it all off as quickly as possible, because I knew these trains did not hang around long at the stations. I stood on the platform alongside the luggage and waited, but could see no sign of Roberto, Tony or Irichelle. The guard blew his whistle as I ran down the platform looking for them. The way things had been going I imagined them still asleep on the train. Just then I saw Roberto on his own and then Tony and Irichelle appeared behind him. Apparently Tony and Irichelle had been involved playing one of their small board games and did not realise that the train was in Newcastle station – once they did realise they both dashed off the train and Irichelle left her board game behind.

I had been joking on with Irichelle saying that it was her turn to lose something as Tony had left his laptop at Miami airport, Roberto had lost his bag at Peterborough, I had lost mine in London; so the board game that she was playing on the train was now on its way to Edinburgh.

At Newcastle station I was expecting the limousine to be there but no limo as this was the first time I had used this guy and he was new to the game. The traffic was chaos at rush hour time so I rang him as Tony went for a coffee. The limo driver said he was not too far away from the station. Just as Tony came back the limo arrived and off we went to the Quality Hotel at Boldon, just a short drive away from the venue at South Shields Temple Park Centre.

We got sorted into our rooms at the hotel and I showered and made a quick dash over to the venue to check things out with Linda and Bryan who were doing the organising that I would normally do. Bryan had dropped off a bag of toiletries for me, as mine had been left in the lost bag. Tony then rang my room and asked if Roberto could borrow them as he had also lost his in the bag lost at Peterborough.

The room at the leisure centre looked good but was very cold and quite dark and the punters were slow to come in; however, everything was underway. Frankie Baggs, the MC, had arrived and the big-screen was set up and those in the room were already watching clips of Roberto's fights to help put them in the mood for his arrival.

With everything in place it was time to go and pick Roberto up. So I drove at top speed back to the hotel and the limousine was outside waiting. In the hotel Roberto was doing his usual and eating in the restaurant without a care in the world. Tony was sitting with him and then Irichelle came down and ordered some food. I let the limo driver know that they would not be too long and then let Bryan inform the MC that we were a little delayed.

I then let Tony and Roberto know that it was time to go as I could imagine the audience getting frustrated with waiting, so off we went, and I told the limo driver to put his foot down. We went in the side door as arranged so that no one would be able to get a glimpse of us arriving. I told Kenny Potts, whose daughter Jennifer was providing the singing entertainment for the night, to play the fanfare, which he put onto one of Jennifer's mini discs.

The fanfare we played for Roberto was one that I personally chose myself after listening to so many. It had a kind of mystique tune to it and a build up to his entrance, which had worked perfectly when he met Ken Buchanan at Newcastle in March. Tony and Irichelle went up onto the stage first and then I held Roberto back and gave Kenny the signal for him to play the fanfare. It worked perfectly and he received a standing ovation as he climbed up the stairs onto the stage, which was quite high up.

I always invited respectable local guests onto the Top table and one I invited this time was Maxie Walsh from the Ex Boxers association of which I was a member. Maxie was chairman of the Tyneside Ex Boxers and was a larger than life guy who was quite a character and told some great tales – and was apparently quite a handy boxer in his day. Maxie was honoured to be sitting alongside Roberto and presented him with a present from the members.

The question and answer session here was the longest of the whole tour. What made it even longer was that there were a couple of jokers in the audience who decided to ask Roberto their questions in Spanish. This was fine at first but the audience did not have a clue what either of them was saying so I got Frankie the MC to move on to questions from the locals.

We then had a couple of guys in the audience who had tattoos of Roberto on their bodies that they wanted him to sign for them so that they could have his signature tattooed over. This had happened at each show on the tour, but these two guys just invited themselves up onto the stage and he signed them there and then. Roberto was fine with this, so I had to be.

After they ran out of questions I took Roberto to the back of the hall where we had the photo and auto screen set up. We were going to call them out table by table, but the queue just filled up and there was not much you could do about it.

Jennifer started her singing spot and entertained those who were awaiting the queue to go down. Jennifer was very good and apart from being an excellent singer she was also a young good looking blonde which went down with the largely-male audience. Roberto signed and posed for photos for over two hours and was great with everybody. The only problems were caused by a few jokers who would have one thing autographed and then go back into the queue and bring something else to sign, although we did inform them that they were only allowed one autograph and one photograph. I do recall watching Roberto play sparring with a youngster that was the son of one of the best boxers to come out of South Shields, Graeme Ahmed. Graeme was delighted with this as Roberto was his favourite boxer.

The limousine arrived for us just after midnight and we set off back to the hotel in Boldon. Two of my pals who worked as security on the night, Paddy and Alan Murray, hitched a ride in the limousine back to the Boldon Lad pub where we drank on a Sunday night and asked Roberto if he would come in for a drink. He normally would have had no problem with this but as our next show was at Cardiff on the Saturday night we had to be up at 5.30 in the morning for the 6.30 flight from Newcastle so we decided to give the pub a miss – we could not afford to miss this flight as it was the only one of the day.

The limousine came on time and off we set for the airport as planned and caught the early flight to Bristol which was as close as we could fly to Cardiff. I sat next to Roberto on the flight and I commented on how small the plane was before we took off. Roberto agreed with me and smiled at me, making the sign of the cross as the engines started up.

On arrival at Bristol we were met by Dave Furnish, the promoter, and the other was Les Clark, the photographer for several boxing establishments. Dave was in a large jeep, which was not quite large enough for us all, so I travelled with Les in his car.

It was about an hour's drive to Cardiff and we stayed in a nice hotel – the Holiday Inn that overlooked the new Millennium Stadium.

We had plenty of time so I went into the centre and found out where the rail station was and informed them about the tickets that I had purchased at Newcastle to travel from Cardiff to London on the Sunday, which were in the lost briefcase. I was hoping they would be able to trace them in the system, but had no joy and had to purchase four more tickets, although I did get them at a reduced price.

I went back to the hotel and give Dave a call and asked to see the venue. Dave kindly drove me over to his club and showed me the venue at St Peters Hall. It was quite small but the tables were dressed very nicely and it certainly looked the part. Dave then drove me back to the hotel and gave me a pack of photos that he wanted Roberto to sign for him and said he would get them back from me when he came to pick us up for the function.

I took a look at the photos and some of them were real collectors' items that I had never seen before. I gave Roberto a ring and asked if it was convenient for me to come along with the photos; he said no problem.

Roberto answered his door just wearing his underwear; he sat on a chair and flicked through the photos and asked me for a pen. He then sounded very excited as he pulled out one of the photos that he had not seen before. The photo was of him very early in his career skipping in a gym with two guys standing alongside him. As he pointed out to me one of them was his late father-in-law and he said that he was going to keep that photo for his wife Fula. I certainly wasn't going to argue over it but I would have to explain it to Dave. One of the other photos was of Roberto and Buchanan at the exact time when the two of them were across the ropes at the time of the supposedly 'low blow'. Roberto said to me: "Take a look at my hands – they are nowhere near his balls." Once again I just agreed with him. I could not believe there were just me and Roberto in the room and he was showing me evidence of one of the greatest controversies in boxing on one of the photos that I had given to him to sign. Dave and Les Clark came up to my room to pick up the photos and we were then all ready to go to the function.

When we got to the venue we were taken through a rear entrance and up some stairs into a waiting room awaiting our call to enter the function room. It was here a strange thing happened. As the time came for us to go through into the main hall, Tony, Roberto and Irichelle were talking and called me over. Tony knew that Ken Buchanan was here and knew that Roberto would be expected to sit next to him on the top table. Tony said to me that he wanted me to go into the room first and sit next to Ken and then Roberto would follow so that I was sat in between them. I put two and two together and realised that this was their way of letting Ken know they felt it was disrespectful for not turning up in Panama especially after they had invited him and paid for his flight and accommodation.

Former World Welterweight champion John H Stracey was the evening's MC and called us into the room. I did as requested and sat next to Ken and I could feel the tension right away from Ken; it was as though he knew he should have attended Roberto's tribute night.

Roberto greeted Ken with a hug and then sat straight back down alongside Tony and me. Roberto went immediately into the question and answer session with the audience and they loved his humour and honesty. We were then taken to the photo session room which was upstairs, but Dave came up after us and asked if we would mind going back down to the top table. Dave wanted this because a lot of the audience had formed a queue for photos and autographs and this would obviously affect his auction income. So we appreciated this and went back down. The auctioneer at the function was a professional one and Roberto found him hilarious and said he was like a horse racing commentator and Roberto had the audience laughing as he stood up and started slapping his backside as though he was riding a horse whilst the auctioneer performed. The auction went on forever as it was for the Johnny Owen memorial fund appeal.

When we eventually went back upstairs for the photos and autographs it was totally disorganised at first as there was just one huge coloured guy there who did not say anything but just stared at people. Things were starting to get out of hand and Dave was nowhere to be seen so Tony asked if I would stand at the door to let them in three at a time, and called the coloured guy over to the table were Roberto was going to sign. This worked a lot better but I felt it was not my job to be standing on the door all night trying to be nice to a lot of drunken Welshmen.

Ken Buchanan was one of the first to come into the room and had a couple of photos taken before saying that he had to leave early. I felt that Ken did not feel comfortable at all. One of Roberto's other opponents Jimmy Batten, also attended the function. Jimmy came into the room, had a photo taken with Roberto and was very obliging and well mannered. Terry Downes also came into the room but had had too much to drink and was trying to talk to anybody but nobody would listen to him. I stood on the door letting them into the room three at a time, and one guy in the queue who was very smartly turned out was none other than Pat Thomas who was a good former British light middleweight champion. Eventually the queue reduced and Dave drove us back to the hotel where we all retired to our rooms.

Dave came to pick us up at about 10am the following morning and gave me a room call asking to see me at reception. He had been paying the hotel bill when he was given a shock by someone's room telephone bill, which was about £400. I knew I had paid my own room calls and but had put it in the contract that any excess to the amount agreed would have to be paid before leaving. Roberto was the guilty one this time and paid Dave with the amount before we left for the rail station.

The train ride was quite comfortable; we sat at a table for four and I showed Tony a few card tricks and my favourite with the matches. At the stop along from Cardiff none other than Jimmy Batten got on the train and I called him over to sit alongside us. Jimmy had fought Roberto in 1980 in Miami and lost a points decision to him. Jimmy and I chatted away for most of the journey and I found him a very charming and interesting guy. He was on his way to London where he was performing as a singer at a club, which was what he was into these days, and he also acted as MC at a lot of boxing shows. Jimmy said to me that he wondered if Roberto remembered boxing him. I said I would ask him, and turned to Roberto who was sitting next to me but dozing in and out of sleep, so I asked Tony who was sitting opposite to pose Jimmy's question. Roberto then asked where the bout had taken place. Jimmy answered that it was in Miami; Roberto then said he did remember and mentioned something to Tony about the fight that Jimmy also remembered. Tony said that Roberto would sometimes forget opponents but would always remember them once you had told him the venue where he had fought them.

Jimmy told me that he went to America because he had his differences with the British boxing board of control and jumped at the chance to fight against Roberto when the chance came. He was then advised by those in the know not to take the fight because Roberto had been previously beaten by Kirkland Laing and Wilfredo Benitez and there was no way that Roberto would lose three fights in a row. Jimmy said it was too good an opportunity to throw away so took the fight in Miami.

He said that he felt the raw strength of Roberto as soon as he hit him with some close range exchanges and he hit like a full middleweight. Into the second round Roberto hit him with some real hard body shots that hurt like hell, and he later found that he had a couple of cracked ribs. Jimmy then decided to box the rest of the contest at long range and was doing ok but not enough to clinch the verdict. His corner men told him that over the last couple of rounds he needed to get in closer and he could maybe get the verdict as Roberto was tiring, but because of his ribs injury there was no way he could mix it with one of the world's hardest body punchers and he lost out to a points verdict.

Jimmy could not believe he had got on the train and just by chance was now sitting alongside the man who most people would ask him about throughout his boxing career; although he had been British light middleweight champion and a good one at that, it was his fight with Roberto Duran that people would ask him about.

I had been in touch with Joe Pyle Jr who was well-known in London's boxing circles and other enterprises, about Roberto coming to London. Joe, along with his friend Pat Morris, had agreed to look after us for our short stay in the capital before we all left from Heathrow airport on the Monday morning.

I let Joe know that we would be arriving at London's Paddington station at around midday on Sunday, and he promised he would be there to meet us. I had been warned by various parties to be very careful in London. Sure enough we were met by Pat Morris at the station and then introduced to Joe and a couple of his henchmen who helped with our luggage and took us to two waiting, top of the range Mercedes cars.

After a short drive we arrived at our hotel which was in Chelsea, West London. After dropping our luggage in our rooms we all went downstairs for a coffee and snack with Joe and his party. We sat for over an hour and the chat was absolutely brilliant with Roberto performing for them and he had them in stitches; for a man who could not speak much English he was amazing, the way that he could get things across to you.

I informed Joe about Roberto's lost passport at Peterborough and how we must go across to Mayfair to the Panamanian Embassy to pick up a replacement passport to enable Roberto to leave the country tomorrow morning (Monday). Joe said that his boys would take us across to the Embassy and run us to wherever we wanted to take a look at whilst we were in the capital and in his company, and that his cars and men were there for us. Joe came across a perfect gentleman.

We went over to the Panamanian embassy where they were delighted to see Roberto who was his charming self with everybody and posed for a few photos with them. After the passport was sorted, Tony and Irichelle asked Pat Morris if he would take them to the Burberry department store. This was based in Selfridges in central London and Joe's drivers knew the surrounding roads like the back of their hands.

I asked one of the drivers if he would run me across to the lost property office and he said no problem. I was hoping that I might be lucky and find my lost briefcase with everything intact and this would make a perfect end to the tour, but it was not to be as when I asked the office was not even open on Sundays and only at certain hours on weekdays.

I went back over to Selfridges and met up with Roberto, Tony and Irichelle. Selfridges is one of the most exclusive department stores in London, and when we first went into it the music was playing to a disco beat and Roberto immediately went into a dance routine. We all had to laugh at him as he could not give a monkey's where he was and his personality was just buzzing all of the time.

Roberto, Pat Morris and I stood for about half an hour awaiting Tony and Irichelle who had disappeared in the store looking around. We waited at the Burberry counter where they wanted to purchase something to take back to the States for a relative. Eventually they turned up, got what they wanted and off we went back to the awaiting drivers in the Mercedes.

Back at the hotel Joe Pyle was standing on the steps outside drinking a can of beer. He greeted us all and said that he had a table booked for us all at a nice restaurant for 7pm. So we said we would get a quick shower and change and meet in the lounge for 7pm. Joe pulled me to one side and asked if it would be ok for Roberto to sign some gloves for him to use for auction to help pay for the hotel bill. I said it was no problem but it would be best to get them done now when we he was in his room. So he told Pat Morris to go and get the gloves and give them to me. Pat went out to the car and came back in with a large bag containing several pairs of gloves, boxing shorts and baseball caps. I went to Roberto's room, explained to him that this was in return for the hotel bill and meals so he put pen to them and signed everything. As he was signing Pat came to the room and gave me his camera to take a few shots for authenticity.

The restaurant Pat took us to was called Montpeliano and was not too far away from the hotel. It had apparently been used by Frank Sinatra when he was in London and was supposedly visited by several of the rich and famous. The manager greeted us all and showed us to our table. It was really exclusive. Joe introduced us all to his business partner Clive Black, who was president of Edel Records and was a charming man. We all ordered our food and the chat was great about a variety of subjects but basically centred on Roberto and Joe exchanging stories about one thing and another, with Roberto having us all in stitches with his banter. Joe's drivers turned up and sat at a table alongside us whilst we eat our final course. One of Joe's men was a novice boxer and Roberto decided to stand up and show him a few moves. This went on for about five minutes and the whole restaurant, which was full, were given an exhibition by a world boxing legend on a few ring moves and counter punches. Roberto did not realise that everybody was watching as his back was turned to them, so when he had finished the whole restaurant gave him a standing ovation.

Joe received a phone call from his dad, Joe Pyle Sr, who had apparently been a member of the notorious Kray twins' gang and agreed that we would go over to a pub to meet him. Joe did mention that there would be a few people there but not in as much as a show or anything.

On the way we popped into a small pub to meet a few of Joe's dad's friends. These were all elderly charming guys who were all there to meet Roberto and had their photos taken with him. I recall showing the photos to a friend when I got back home and he named them all as big players in the London underworld. I did not have a clue who any of them were, but Roy Shaw, Freddie Foreman and Joe's dad were there; however, they were all very kind to us and we never paid for anything.

The drivers took us all over to a pub by the name of R & J's in Twickenham. As we entered the pub you could hear over a microphone 'please welcome ROBERTO DURAN'. We then went in to the sound of disco music and to the light of photographer's flashes.

The pub probably had about a hundred or so people in but it was quite relaxed, although Roberto had his photo taken with everybody in the place. We met all the regulars and Joe's dad and his associates. A disc jockey played some music and everybody was having a good time. Roberto liked the record 'Stand by me' and asked the DJ to play it for him. One of the tunes that came on was one of the Santana rhythm beats and I could not help but notice Irichelle dancing to the beat as she stood next to me – you could tell she had a natural rhythm about her.

One of Joe Pyle's friends came over to us and he was a guy in his 60s who looked really frightening. He took a glass of wine and balanced it on his head whilst moving to the beat of the music; he then unbelievably went down onto the floor and performed ten perfect press ups and then stood up without spilling a drop. We were all amazed and Roberto was laughing his head off at him. It was getting late by now and we knew we had an early start tomorrow so we requested to go back to the hotel.

On the way back we all got in the same car with Roberto in the front and Tony, Irichelle and me in the back seat of the Mercedes. Roberto started his shouting and screaming antics and began to have a go at Tony who apparently was going through a tough time with his wife. Roberto went on and on and had the driver in stitches, but Tony just laughed it off till we got back to the hotel.

I packed my case as soon as we got back and rang reception for an early morning call for 7am. Roberto's flight back to the States was at 11am but they had to be at the airport for about 8am so as to get the clearance with Roberto's passport.

We all had breakfast together but Irichelle could not manage anything, as she was feeling rough from the previous night. Joe's men arrived and off we went on our way to the airport which was about a half-hour run. At the airport we went over to the American Airlines desk and got Roberto's passport clearance and then stood in the queue to go through into the waiting lounge. Irichelle was not feeling well at all now and Roberto was laughing at her and taking the mickey out of her saying that last night she was very happy and dancing but now her head was very sore.

The time came for them to depart and they all gave me a huge hug before leaving for the departure lounge. I stood and watched as they ascended up the escalator thinking that this would be the last time I would see them all. At the top Roberto stood still and turned and waved to me, just as he had done at Newcastle, and I got the same gut feeling inside of me as he disappeared and I made my way across to the other Terminal.

IRICHELLE DURAN, MARTYN & ROBERTO DURAN AT SOUTH SHIELDS, 2002

JOE PYLE JNR AND MARTYN, LONDON, OCTOBER 2002

ROBERTO PLAYING BONGOS, SHEFFIELD, 2002

*VIVIENNE SANDERS, KEVIN SANDERS (PROMOTER) AND
ROBERTO DURAN, PETERBOROUGH, 2002*

ROBERTO, TONY AND IRICHELLE WITH PROMOTER GLYN RHODES, SHEFFIELD, 2002

JOE PYLE SNR AND MARTYN, LONDON, 2002

ANOTHER TOUR

I was contacted again by Tony on 2 April 2003 enquiring about the possibility of Roberto making an appearance in Scotland or other parts of the UK during the year. I let him know that the Scottish promoter was interested and I would enquire about any more. Tony suggested a tour with Iran Barkley whom Roberto had defeated during an epic battle for the world Middleweight title in 1989, but I informed him that I did not think that it would sell because Barkley had not had the exposure over here, and also the requested fee was too much.

I chased up Norrie Sweeney from Scotland who had made a previous enquiry about Roberto's appearance. He said that he would still like to feature Roberto, so I thought I would put an advert in Boxing News and see if there was any demand, although I doubted there would be due to it being so close to the previous 2002 tour.

The two enquiries I received were from Glyn Rhodes, which surprised me as he had already featured Roberto, and from former world welterweight champion John H Stracey who said that he was back in London now and that he and his partner would stage Roberto in London provided they had exclusivity in London and that his colleague Ken Purchase would also feature Roberto at Telford, near Birmingham. Norrrie said that he could only feature Roberto if it were a Friday or Saturday night and that he would have to check whether it might clash with one of Scott Harrison's fights.

Tony was obviously keen to come over again but said they would like to come for at least four shows and agreed a fee for that. With John H wanting two shows and Norrie and Glyn, it looked as though it should be ok for the four shows. Norrie finally contacted me to say that his show must be on a Friday night. Glyn Rhodes wanted the Wednesday so I contacted John H and asked him what nights he would like to take. John then hit me with the news that he had lost his sponsor and that he was also not happy with the contents of the contract I had sent him, although this was the same contract that all six promoters had worked to on Roberto's previous tour of 2002.

I then received a call and then a fax from Ken Purchase who was a colleague of John H Stracey's and John had already sent him the contract. Ken said he was interested in featuring Roberto after a successful show with Ken Norton recently but would not sign or work to the contract in its present state. I informed Ken that it was the same contract that all six shows on Roberto's previous tour had worked to. I then received the contract back and signed from Norrie Sweeney and from Glyn Rhodes, so that was two shows finalised.

I advertised in Boxing News and tried an old trick to say that there was only one show date left for staging Roberto.

I then received a call from Eric Ragonesi who, like Ken Purchase, was from Telford. Eric let me know that he owned a nightclub there and was looking to feature Roberto there and obviously make his money from the bar takings. I said I would send him the contract and he could then decide. I slightly altered some of the wording on the contract to make it less Americanised but still kept the major clauses intact.

I then received a call the very next day from Ken Purchase to say he was still interested and would I send him the new contract to look over; I also informed him that I had been contacted by Eric Ragonesi. Ken did not appear too happy about this as they were both in the same area.

I sent the contract to Ken and he immediately called me back saying he was now satisfied with it and would forward me his deposit which arrived that same week.

I then had to let Eric know about this and he agreed that business was business and it was a case of Ken had returned his contract signed along with his deposit so I had no option but to confirm it. Ken confirmed that he wanted the Tuesday night. So this meant that with the Tuesday, Wednesday and Friday evenings booked I needed just one more show to confirm the tour.

As Roberto had been up in this area twice before there was no way that I could do anything with him in the Newcastle area, but then I thought what about Sunderland which always had a large amateur boxing fraternity.

I contacted Sunderland football club's ground The stadium of light and asked to speak to their functions organiser. It turned out to be a charming girl by the name of Stephanie. Stephanie asked if I would go over and meet her and her catering manager and let them know some details about Roberto Duran.

I went over and met up with Stephanie who informed me that she was leaving the Stadium to go and work at Darlington FC, and she introduced me to a Scottish girl by the name of Barbara who was taking over from her and wanted to know about the possibility of Roberto coming to Sunderland. They appeared to be all for it and Stephanie said she would contact their corporate customers and put the feelers out amongst them. I spoke to the sports editor at the local Sunderland Echo newspaper and asked him to give it a mention. Over the following weekend I had quite a few enquiries about Roberto's appearance in Sunderland so I decided to give it a go and go for it on the Saturday night to make up the fourth show date.

I contacted Tony Gonzalez about this and let him know that I would put a show on but this would have to be at a reduced fee, as I was only putting it on to make the tour possible for them. He did agree to this and gave me a reduced fee, but it was not by much.

I received quite a few calls from Eric Ragonesi enquiring if Roberto was still coming to his area and I informed him that Ken Purchase was now definitely going ahead with his show.

Out of the blue I received a call from Leicester from a guy by the name of Gra Burt who had attended the show at Newcastle in which I featured Roberto and Ken Buchanan. Gra said that he and his partner Paul McHugh were interested in featuring Roberto at Leicester but as he was due to go on holiday he would give me Paul's contact number.

I contacted Paul and sent him the contract to look over but

he did inform me that he could not do anything without Gra's approval.

So I informed Tony of the new enquiries and said we would have to wait to confirm things. Tony was not as demanding with time limits this time, although he had demanded a slightly higher fee per show than the previous tour. Tony also said that Roberto had been more than generous with the amount of autographs he had signed on the previous tour and that he would like to put a limit on this and that any of the promoters who wanted private signing sessions would have to compensate Roberto accordingly. I did make sure that this was inserted into their contracts but I did point out to Tony that photos and autographs were what the fans were paying for and we should not forget this as the fee was increased from the last tour.

I contacted Paul McHugh who came across as a smashing guy as did his friend Gra, and asked him to contact me as soon as Gra arrived back as time was now running out for deposits to be made - and also there was only the one night left available. Gra contacted me the following day and after assuring him about a few things he said that they would definitely go ahead with featuring Roberto at Leicester.

This meant that I now had five shows from Tuesday through to Saturday. I then had a call from Eric Ragonesi wondering if it would be at all possible for Roberto to come to a small gathering of his family and friends at his club on the afternoon before Ken Purchase's show. I told him this would not be possible as we were in London then. He then suggested the following Sunday evening but I said that I would have to speak to Tony and find out how long they were staying in the UK.

I received the flight Itinerary from Tony which let me know that they would be arriving on Monday morning and leaving the following Monday morning.

This then meant that I would have to accommodate them for seven nights although they were only doing five shows.

So I then contacted Eric and let him know that Roberto could be available for the Sunday evening if he wanted him. He said he was interested but wanted Roberto at a reduced fee as it would be half of the appearance time quoted in the contract. I said I would ask Tony about this but did not see any problems with it. On putting Eric's request to Tony he replied that it would be fine but wanted a little more than half of the fee, which became typical of him.

Eric agreed to the fee and as he wanted to stage Roberto so much, I was glad he was getting him at his club, the 42 Club.

So the tour was now set up – starting at Telford on the Tuesday, Sheffield Wednesday, Leicester Thursday, Glasgow Friday, Sunderland Saturday and then back down to Telford on the Sunday evening. So I now had to go ahead with travel and accommodation arrangements.

I contacted Tony to let him know the final bookings for the tour and then asked him to give me their flight itinerary as soon as possible.

Tony replied some time later with the itinerary which confirmed that they were arriving on the Monday and leaving on the following Monday. This meant that I had to provide overnight accommodation for them in London on the Monday evening.

I contacted my London pal Joe Pyle and told him the situation and he said no problem, that he would look after Roberto for the Monday and meet us at the airport when he arrived, so I was more than happy about that.

Joe called me back later and asked what I thought about Roberto taking part in a boxing match that would be what he called "a put up bout". I said I would mention it to them and then he could discuss it with them himself when they arrived. At first this sounded a little crazy to me but when they started talking about the money that could be involved it might be of interest to Roberto, obviously depending on his financial state.

So the tour was now set and I had to begin a serious push with the Sunderland show. After being in touch with the local press I received quite a few enquiries from the area which surprised me a little, given that Roberto had been in the north east twice already. I found that some punters would only attend shows within their own area and did not wish to travel outside their own towns. Sunderland also had six Amateur boxing clubs that I targeted, although only members from two of them eventually booked.

I found by experience that to get the media attention you usually have to put a pair of free tickets up for grabs and it also helps if you give the reporters or radio announcers a couple. This can still work out cheaper than advertising space which can cost a small fortune.

Now I could get to work on the travel and accommodation arrangements. It was up to each show promoter to provide overnight accommodation in a decent hotel at or near the venue, and to hopefully provide the transport from the previous evening's show, as with the last tour. I decided to make a start with booking accommodation for the Saturday night in Sunderland, which gave me my first major problem.

On enquiring at Sunderland's Quality hotel, which would have been ideal as Roberto had stayed there previously and we had been given a great deal there, I was informed by Sandra Devlin that the hotel had been fully booked for a long time because that was the weekend of the Great North Run.

The Great North Run was an annual half marathon attended by some 40,000 runners from across the world, and was a run I had previously taken part in myself. The run mainly attracted novices fundraising for various organisations and I had actually taken part in five Great North Runs and recall doing the first ever one in 1981 when only 12,000 runners took part and the entry fee was just £1.50. The last one I took part in was in 1996 when I raised money for the Alzheimer's research fund, which is a dreadful disease that attacks and kills off the brain cells and eventually ended my father's life.

I rang every large hotel in Sunderland and Newcastle, and not one of them had accommodation. I contacted Barbara Bewick at the Stadium of Light and explained the situation to her and she gave me the number of a couple of places used by the Sunderland football team's opponents on match days. These were also fully booked. I then contacted the tourist information at both areas who gave me the same story, but that they would take my details for any cancellations although they could not promise anything and that they were now booking runners into accommodations at Hexham and Durham which was too far out of the area.

I was busy building an extension onto my own house that would end up with us having extra bedrooms. If pushed, this was going to be my only option, so I decided to press on with it. Although the contract stated that accommodation had to be a 4/5 star hotel, I knew Roberto would be fine with anywhere half decent, after seeing some of the poorer parts of Panama.

After hitting many spells of bad weather I knew that although I had the main part of the building of my extension up, there was no way that it was going to be ready in time for September 21st, so I knew I had to find somewhere to put them up.

I rang the Longship pub hotel in Hebburn, which was a place I had used to put up former world light heavyweight champion John Conteh and also world heavyweight title challenger Earnie Shavers after previous functions. Unfortunately they were also fully booked but the girl gave me the number of her friend in South Shields who also ran a guesthouse.

I spoke to a girl by the name of Karen, informed her of my problem and let her know that it was a celebrity boxer by the name of Roberto Duran. Karen had never heard of him but said she would speak to her husband when he returned home.

The following day her husband Paul Redfern rang me and said that although he was fully booked he would try and make some changes to accommodate such a legend at his Tuckers Inn guest house in Beach Road, South Shields. I arranged with Paul to take a look at the place a week or so later.

Tuckers Inn was based in Beach Road, South Shields, not far from the Town Hall. On the notice board in the garden it states that contractors are welcome which straight away gives you the impression that it's not going to be up to much. Paul answered the door and took me and Linda in to show us around. The entrance hallway was much like a building site entrance, but Paul assured me it would be all ok by the time Roberto came. The room he showed us where Roberto would be staying was fine with a large double bed and Tony's room would be similar but upstairs on the first floor. Paul and Karen were both charming and we had a laugh with them. I informed Paul that it would be ok and that I would keep in touch.

On leaving Linda said to me that it was not too bad but I should still look for somewhere better as when I went to Panama they did put me in a 5-star hotel. The problem was there was nowhere else available. So I provisionally booked Tuckers Inn and said I would call back when the work was finished.

With Roberto's flight due in at 9.50am it meant that I was going to have to be in London early, so I called to ask if there were any places on the 6.30 flight from Newcastle to London. I was informed that the only seats available were £200. I then checked out the trains which were only £70 return but the early morning one would not get me there on time. I decided to leave the evening before and stay overnight in London, and travel across to Heathrow on the Monday morning.

Bryan dropped me off at Newcastle rail station and I was informed the London train was on Platform two so I made my way across and jumped on board. I then overheard someone saying that this was a Virgin train, and I knew that I should be travelling on GNER. I jumped off and asked one of the porters who then informed me that the GNER train to London was now leaving from a different platform. So over I went and climbed on board. Once settled I went for a walk down to the buffet carriage and bumped into an old primary school friend and one of the best footballers to come out of Jarrow, Anthony McCaffery. Anthony was travelling to Doncaster to visit his brother so I bought a couple of cans of beer for us and we chatted over old times, and had a laugh.

The train was due into King's Cross at 12 midnight but when we got near Peterborough there was a power failure on the overhead lines so we came to a complete standstill.

The train eventually got started but did not arrive at King's Cross until 3am, some three hours late. We were informed that because of this delay we would be provided with free taxis to our destination. By the time the queue went down it was 3.30am. The digs I had booked were at Victoria so I thought it may be it best to ask if the cab would take me over to Heathrow airport, then at least I was there and did not have the following morning rush hour traffic to worry about.

The cab journey took around an hour as another couple also from the delayed train joined me and were dropped off somewhere on the route to Heathrow. I finally arrived at Heathrow around 4.30am. I found a place on some seating that looked comfortable and tried to get a couple of hours' sleep. The cleaning machines put an end to anyone trying to get some sleep as they start up around 6am with their noisy motors. The cafés open around that time anyway so I decided to have some breakfast and read a couple of morning papers. The time was dragging like hell but their flight was on schedule by the timetable display and due to arrive at 9.50am.

At around 8.45am I received a call from Joe Pyle Jr letting me know that he was just leaving home with his boys and should be across within an hour. Joe was a great guy to have in your company and was very well respected in the London area and always a man of his word.

Roberto's flight was due in soon and I thought about the first time that I was waiting on Roberto at Newcastle airport when I was sweating wondering whether he would turn up or not. This time it was not so bad but you still had the worry in the back of your mind.

I received a call from Joe Pyle to tell me he was at the airport and wondering where I was? After informing him he quickly touched me on the shoulder from behind, and we both had a laugh about it. Joe was about mid thirties, always dapper and had a lot of respect in the London area. He reminded me about the birth of his twins who were now a few months old.

Anyway before large crowds started coming through the exit terminal and I asked one of them what flight he was off and he said the Miami flight, so now the sweat was on looking out for Roberto and Tony amongst the hundreds passing through.

I mentioned to Joe this was the time I worry most, but just as I said that I caught a glimpse of Roberto and Tony. I gave a wave and Roberto caught my eye first and nudged Tony. We all greeted each other and Joe took us out to meet his boys. We were introduced to Perry, a massive guy, and Bobby, an ex pro who now took part in unlicensed shows.

I jumped into Joe's plush Jag and Roberto and Tony got into a black Range Rover which Bobby drove.

We drove across to the Marriott hotel at Regents Park which was a plush five star hotel. We checked in and Joe called me over to ask if I could show a credit card at the hotel's request as he did not use one. I then had visions of me getting a massive hotel bill but I had total confidence that Joe would stick to our private agreement. Porters carried our luggage into our rooms and then Joe asked if we wanted to get a bite and have a drink, to which we all agreed. Perry drove us across to a small bar cafe which was run by a pal of Joe. It was a mild day so we all sat outside and had a coffee and a sandwich and a good chat.

Roberto suggested that he was a little tired so Joe said that he would take us back to the hotel and we could get a couple of hours' rest. Back at the hotel Roberto called me over in private and asked me if I could get him something which I did not understand. He then took off his New York baseball cap to reveal a lot of grey hairs amongst his head of thick jet black hair. So what he wanted was some black dye to put on. I said no problem and took a stroll to the local shops to see what I could get for him. I explained to the lady what it was for and she said that 'Just for men' should be ok. So there I was buying some hair dye for one of the most ferocious and macho boxers of all time. I went back to the hotel, gave Roberto a knock and passed the bottle to him, for which he was very grateful. I went back to my room and rested for a while before taking a shower. Joe gave me a call and said he would meet me down at the bar with his boys. I went down to meet Joe who ordered a couple of drinks and we were then joined by Perry, Bobby and Ricky English, an ex pro who now ran a gym in the area. I gave Tony and Roberto a call to let them know we were awaiting them. Roberto came down first and started his banter with us all; it was not long before he had them all laughing with his carry on. Roberto, although he does not speak much English, had a unique way of getting across to you, and understanding what you were saying. When you were in his company he always had the chair, which was unbelievable for a Spanish-speaking guy, and somehow always got his point across to you, most of it being clean gags and fun.

I then received a call from Frankie Baggs, whom I had booked to be our MC at Sunderland, to say that he was ill and could not make it. I thought just what I needed a few days beforehand. I immediately contacted Martin Emmerson from Radio Newcastle whose wife had let me know that he would be interested in doing some work at my sporting dinners. Martin said he would check his workload out that week and get back to me as soon as he could.

Now that we were all ready we got into the cars with Perry and Bobby driving. They drove us through London's West End and on the way Roberto asked if he could get a couple of photos of the sights. We were near the London wheel and Roberto stood alongside with a few of the boys and I took some photos for him, for which he thanked me.

Joe took us to a restaurant called the Palace which was a plush, large restaurant that was quite high up with brilliant views. We all sat at a huge table and ordered our food. I had a laugh with Perry whom I sat next to as when I asked him what he was having he said "that stuff there," pointing on the menu, "because it's the only stuff I can f........ understand," as a lot of the menu was foreign. One of Joe's business pals picked up the bill and I'll bet it was easily three figures. After the meal we were driven to a pub run by Freddie Foreman's son.

In the pub that night it was like a rogues' gallery with only invited guests who included Joe Pyle Sr, Freddie Foreman and Roy 'Pretty boy' Shaw who looked in amazingly good shape for his age. They had a huge coloured guy on the door who must have been over seven foot tall and three foot wide. We all had a laugh at the pub and Roberto posed for photos with them all.

We left the pub after a couple of hours and then headed to a club in the West End where we were treated like royalty on arrival. Once inside I ended up sitting next to Roberto with Joe Pyle Sr on the other side of him. Drinks were ordered for us and then the fun started. A beautiful young girl with very little on had been sent over to dance for Roberto. The club was, of course, a table-dancing club, where girls came over to you and offered to dance for you after which they expected you to put some paper money in their tights or knickers. The odd thing about this was that we were getting it all for free, and they just kept coming over to Roberto and performing for him, beauty after beauty.

As they danced in front of Roberto each of them would always bend right over and push their arse close to him; as they did this I would let out a great rasper for a laugh. Roberto was absolutely in stitches and found it hilarious, to the point where he just could not stop laughing, and for days after he would joke on about it to me.

We left the club about 2.30am and headed back to the hotel. Joe Pyle Sr gave me his mobile number and asked for my number, as he wanted to know when we would be back at the hotel as he wanted Roberto to sign something for him. Back at the hotel we sat for a bit while Joe had his signing done and he presented Roberto with one of his autobiographies to take back to Panama.

The following morning I received a call from Ken Purchase who was staging the next show at Telford. Ken asked our whereabouts in London and suggested that he would come and pick us up in the limousine. As I already had train tickets to get to Birmingham I let Ken know that it would be better if he picked us up at Birmingham station, as the traffic in London was too congested and it might take too long to get there.

I booked a cab to take us to Euston station for our train to

Birmingham. Roberto and Tony went for a burger while they were waiting. On the train there was plenty of room so we took a double seat each and I sat across the aisle from Roberto and opposite an elderly guy who informed me that he was travelling to visit his son in Wales but would catch his connection at Birmingham.

Roberto put on his headphones, put in his disc and started singing along with the music. This was nothing new to me now but the elderly guy opposite said that my friend appeared to be enjoying himself. I pulled a pack of dominoes out of my bag and asked him if he fancied a game, to which he agreed.

As we played Roberto's chants got louder and louder and my dominoes opponent laughed. As Roberto usually had his eyes closed when listening and singing to his music, I asked my friend if he knew who he was. He said no and I then informed him that he was a famous boxer by the name of Roberto Duran. He said he had never heard of him, and asked if he was Spanish. I told him he was from Panama.

My elderly opponent was beating me almost every game. When I informed Roberto of this he asked why. I said that he was very good at it and Roberto laughed and then put his headphones back on. I threw Roberto a copy of the boxing news over; he glanced at a few pictures and photos in the paper and then chucked it back over to me as though he were not interested.

I was getting constant calls from Ken Purchase who was awaiting us at Birmingham station and was probably sweating as we were delayed for nearly an hour at Coventry.

At the station I met up with Ken who also had with him former world WBC super middleweight champion Richie Woodhall, and a couple of other guys.

Ken was about late forties and seemed a flamboyant character dressed in jeans and t-shirt and had probably come straight from working at his beer sales business. The limousine awaited us and I sat alongside Richie who was typically down to earth like most of the boxing fraternity and overwhelmed to be in the car with Roberto. Roberto once again put his music on and sang along to it, which they all had a laugh at. Ken put some of his Elvis Presley tapes on and let us hear his own voice which was actually quite good.

The venue Ken used was a Travelodge at Telford which was very big with a massive function room that probably sat about 400 people. Once Ken showed me to our rooms he asked me if Roberto would sign some items for him. I said to show them to me and then I would consult with Roberto. At Ken's room he had all kinds of pictures, prints and gloves, amounting to about 30 items. Tony had insisted with me that Roberto wanted to be compensated for any extra private signing sessions which I made sure was inserted within the contract and knew there would be a problem with this many items, as some of the promoters were going a little over the top.

I contacted Tony and asked him to come and take a look at them and he immediately informed Ken that Roberto would not sign that amount for free. Ken was not too happy about this and let us know, but I did tell him Roberto was ok signing a couple of items but not that many. Ken said that Ken Norton had not had a problem signing anything when he had featured him, but I said Duran was a different kettle of fish.

Tony called me and asked my views and I suggested putting a fee on them to keep the peace, but when he told Ken the fee it was still too much. Eventually I suggested to Tony to come down a little although deep down I was not too bothered because I was getting nothing from it anyway. They came to a settlement figure eventually but I got the impression neither was too happy about it.

I then asked Ken for the payment. He came to the room with it but when I counted it out it was way short of the required amount. After the hassle with the items to be signed this was all we needed. Ken rang the bank in front of me and informed them they had given him the wrong amount. I then spoke to the girl who agreed with me the dollar equivalent that it should have been. Ken realised there had been a mistake and said he would get the extra dollars as soon as possible, I did let him know that I had encountered a similar problem on the last tour and Roberto would not make his appearance until it was correct. Somehow the dollars eventually appeared and everything was fine.

Tony then came to my room and asked if I would go to a department store with him as Roberto had not brought a shirt with him, so needed to buy a couple. As the time was now 6.30pm I said there was no way that any shops would be open now, but I had brought five white shirts with me so Roberto could use one those. Tony replied that Roberto was a lot bulkier than me and they would not fit him, but I suggested he tried anyway. Sure enough when Roberto came down to the function he had my white shirt on but with the neck open and a white tee shirt underneath. Roberto was one of those guys who looked good in whatever he had on even though at times he would just put anything on that came close to fitting him.

The function room was huge and must have had about 400 punters in. Ken MC'd the show himself and went round table by table having a bit of banter with those on it; this seemed to take forever. Roberto was then introduced and the questions started coming with the help of John H Stracey who helped out with the master of ceremonies.

Ken had a huge amount of items that he auctioned, and there was little time spent on the photo session with Roberto, which did not bother him.

At the function a small bald guy came over and introduced himself as none other than Eric Ragonesi, who had booked Roberto for the Sunday at his club. Eric was very sociable and we had a laugh together. He asked if we were going anywhere afterwards and I said we would go with the flow as Roberto liked the nightclubs.

We were driven to a club owned by some of the underworld of Telford and looked after in there. It was a dark and overcrowded joint with loud music and a few dancers, one of whom gave Roberto a private dance.

We left at about 2.30am and were driven home by an Asian guy who let us know he had just served a five year stretch for shooting some other gang member.

The following morning I had breakfast and then sat with John H Stracey and his wife Kathy who was very beautiful and spoke several languages. John took me to his car to show me some framed pictures he had in the boot. The pictures were all of famous world champions and most were signed. John also ran some kind of business in which he dealt with memorabilia.

Memorabilia is quite profitable but it is not something that I am personally attracted to although I do have gloves signed to me personally by most of the champions that I have featured over the years and have them on show at home; and I always make sure I have a programme from my own shows personally signed to my daughter Joy, for her keepsake when she is old enough to understand. However I would never purchase any memorabilia unless it was signed in front of me or was from a genuine reliable source.

Later Roberto and Tony came down and ordered some sandwiches as they were, as usual, too late for breakfast, and, as usual, had no track of time for anything.

The waitress was good enough to make up a few sandwiches for them and some coffee; John and Kathy left with Ken and his wife. Ken Buchanan came over and sat with me and Roberto as Tony had disappeared to use the toilet. Ken was laughing when he said to Roberto that he was tired of people asking him over the years about why the return fight with Roberto never came off, and he then said to me and Roberto that he never wanted to fight him again, as the first fight was hard enough! Then Roberto stood up and laughed and gave Ken a big hug, and said that he was his amigo.

I had to pinch myself as there I was sitting with two legends in boxing joking with each other over one of the most talked about bouts in the history of the lightweight division.

We said our goodbyes to Ken Purchase and his family, shook hands and then promoter Glyn Rhodes turned up in a beautiful white limousine to take us across to Sheffield for the next show on the Wednesday evening.

Glyn was his usual self and as he had been in the game about the same length of time as myself but had opted to go into the professional ranks both as a boxer and now a manager and promoter. Glyn turned up with his pal Steve Sidebottom whom I had also met previously.

Sheffield was about a couple of hours' drive so we all got settled and had a chat about this and that and then Roberto decided to put his music on and started singing his head off, much to the amusement of Glyn and Steve.

Roberto went into his small backpack and asked Steve if he would like a walnut sweet from Panama that he promised would be very nice. Steve appeared to be having trouble with the taste of whatever Roberto had given him, as he put his hand into his mouth and took a look at the so called sweet that he had been chewing on.

Roberto seemed very interested in the look on Steve's face when he opened the sweet to reveal a tiny condom inside of its shell. We were all in fits of laughter when we saw the condom but Steve took it all in good fun.

We were then stuck in a traffic jam for about 30 minutes so we decided to stop off at a service station and hope the jam would be cleared by the time we came out.

We finally arrived at Sheffield about 5.00pm and Glyn asked if we would pop into his gym as we had done on the previous visit. Roberto sparred with a couple of the kids and posed for photos with them.

Always our contract stated that Roberto be paid his dollars before his appearance, so I contacted Glyn to remind him of this. Glyn as usual was running around like a blue-arsed fly organising everything, but then let me know that he had forgotten to bring the dollars with him. I reminded him that this might cause a problem with Tony and he said that he would make sure that they were at the function.

At the function I once again reminded Glyn and he said that his partner Steve had the dollars with him. I caught up with Steve who asked me to go into a private room with him. On counting out the dollars I let Steve know that he was short by way of a couple of thousand. I ran over the contract with Steve and he agreed that they had made a mistake. There was no way he could get the right amount of dollars now but promised to get them first thing the following morning. Luckily Tony and Roberto had already begun eating at the top table so I was not going to let them know just in case they walked out, but I knew Glyn and Steve would stick by their word.

Glyn had invited a lot of the British champions to his show and put them all on the top table with Roberto in the centre of them.

Roberto joked with them all, some of whom he had met before but others were overwhelmed by his banter. They included John Conteh, Alan Minter, Charlie Magri, Earnie Shavers, Richie Woodhall, John H Stracey and the evening's MC Steve Holdsworth from Eurosport.

Glyn asked me if I would mind sitting on one of the floor tables as opposed to the top table. I did not mind this and sat alongside some of the amateur coaches from Glyn's gym, and had a good chat with them about the state of the Amateurs and how things differed from region to region.

Tony asked me if it would be OK for him to sell some of his own photos of Roberto and also auction some posters of Roberto's last world title bout in Panama, I said to him that he would have to ask Glyn about this, although I personally did not agree with it as he was receiving a fee already for Roberto's appearance.

Glyn must have agreed to let Tony sell the posters as all three of them were auctioned off at the function and each met their reserve price.

One of the guys was a member of the Leeds ex-boxers association and I had met up with him previously at the Tyneside EBA of which I was a member. He showed me his personal autograph book which was filled with boxing legends' names from across the world, but the one he did not have was Roberto's, so he tore out a page and asked if I would get it for him and send it on to him. I did this the very next day for him.

As the night went on I realised there would be a problem and reminded Glyn of the time factor, but he said not to worry about it. The reason for this was that Roberto was only contracted to make a four hour appearance, and the dinner was now running on to well over two hours. After the dinner, Steve introduced a big screen film show with highlights of the best contests of every fighter on the top table. This ran for over 40 minutes and finished with a clip of Glyn himself in action during his pro career. After this the girls went round with the raffle tickets which again took up about half an hour and they then decided to have a 'true or false' boxing quiz. Whilst all of this was going on I was taking a look at Roberto and could not help but notice how uneasy he was and although he kept smiling he looked bored.

Roberto was the type of guy who had to be busy doing something, just as he was in his fighting style, throwing bunches of punches at his opponents. I knew it was a bad idea to bring him in for the dinner which seemed to take forever. They then decided to start with the question and answer session, which once again should have been earlier due to a lot of the punters being now well served with beer, and some ridiculous questions coming from some of them. This session took us up to nearly midnight, which was now over the four hour period agreed by contract.

All of the champions were then taken to a table at the back of the hall for fans to queue for photos and autographs. This was going to take forever and after about ten minutes Tony came over to me and said that Roberto was well over his time and was going to leave. I had to let Glyn know this, and he was not too happy about it, but Tony also let him know. Glyn let Tony know if that's what Roberto wanted to do then let him do it.

So that was that; Roberto came from the table and made his way to the awaiting limousine outside. The fans were not happy about this at all, but made do with the rest of the champions who were left at the table. Tony insisted that Glyn had got it wrong on the night with his show format. I had to agree with him, but it was not the actual format was wrong, it was just that everything took much longer than expected.

After the show I went back to the hotel and had a couple of beers and a laugh with Charlie Magri, Richie Woodhall, and Alan Minter and also had a chat with Jason Barker who was one of Glyn's main sponsors whom I found to be a nice guy. But there was no sign of Glyn, Tony or Roberto.

The following morning I tried to contact Glyn but there was no reply, I eventually got in contact with his partner Steve Sidebottom as I had to sort out the missing dollars with him. Steve was fine about this and I met up with him after he had been to his bank for the correct amount of dollars and he apologised for the mix up.

Tony contacted me to try and get the money and photos off Glyn from the function. I said I would give him Glyn's number as I was no part of the deal and did not know anything about the photos, which had apparently been given to Glyn at the function.

Glyn then contacted me to say that he did not have any idea of the whereabouts of the photos and that the money owed from the auction of the posters would be mailed to Tony. He also let me know that deep down he was not really bothered about it, because of Roberto walking out of the function, and the amount of complaints he had been receiving.

I let Tony know this, but he was still adamant that he was due the money and the photos, but all I could tell him was what Glyn had already relayed to me.

I booked a cab from the Sheffield hotel to the train station and booked our tickets to go to Leicester. The train ride to Leicester was only an hour or so.

At the Leicester station we were met by the promoter Gra Burt and his pal Paul McHugh and then by none other than the former world middleweight title challenger Tony Sibson.

Tony took me, Roberto and Tony over to his black Range Rover jeep and sorted our luggage for us. I sat in the front with him and what a real nice down to earth lad he was, just as I had expected. Once he had retired from the sport Tony stayed clear of the limelight and never made any TV appearances or got involved in any media work. He let me know that he was still involved in the house building and renovating work and was moving to the south-west of England.

Tony had the perfect build for a middleweight with one of the best left hooks in the game and was well known for destroying Alan Minter in their British title fight. I let him know that I had been with Alan the night before and he spoke highly of him. I always recall when Tony fought Minter that it was never shown on TV because of some sponsorship deal regarding a name that was on Minter's shorts. They both told me the story behind it, which apparently cost them both a lot of money. Tony went on to challenge the awesome Marvelous Marvin Hagler for the world middleweight crown in Boston in 1983 but was stopped in the sixth round by a punch perfect Hagler although Tony gave a good account of himself.

Tony drove us to a Travelodge where we dropped our luggage off and they then drove us to a pub in the middle of a council estate, to meet up with a local press photographer.

There were only a couple of people in the pub. We sat and had a coffee before a young female photographer called us to a room at the back of the pub where there was an old punch bag hanging up. Roberto posed for a few photos with Gra, Paul and Tony Sibson.

Tony told me that he was honoured to be in Roberto's company and said he was always one of his favourite fighters. Tony said that although he would attend the function he could not stay too long as he was off on holiday to Spain the following morning.

The function was held at a workingmen's club bang in the middle of a council estate. Gra picked me up first and said he would call back for Roberto and Tony. He explained his show format me and said he would show clips of Roberto's fights on the big-screen followed by some comedy with Nipper Thomas and then bring Roberto in. Gra then asked if I would MC it for him? I said that I would rather not, but if he was pushed I would do it for him. I spoke with the comedian Nipper Thomas about this and he said he would do most of it but asked me to introduce Roberto as the audience would just laugh at him doing it.

The function room was large enough to put around 300 in but there still appeared to be plenty of seats about, so Gra put the big-screen clips on and then I let him know that I did not want a reoccurrence of last night's show with Roberto sitting doing nothing for hours, and that he would rather be busy, signing or posing for photos with fans.

Nipper then took over and told a few tales along with some corny jokes. Most of the audience must have either seen Nipper before or knew of him, as they did not seem to take much notice of him although I personally found him really funny. He was only a small guy and just rolled up his shirtsleeves and mingled in with the audience cracking gags as he went around. He also cracked a few using Roberto as his back up, but I honestly don't think he had ever heard of Roberto before the show, and kept saying Duran Duran (as in the pop group) would be coming soon.

Gra gave me the signal to let me know that Roberto had arrived and Tony Sibson also took his place on the top table, so I grabbed the mike and did my best to use an entrance similar to Dave Greener's at Newcastle: "Please welcome the former Lightweight... welterweight... junior middleweight... middleweight... and super middleweight champion of the world, ROBERTO Hands of stone DURAN".

The audience gave Roberto a standing ovation and I then said that we would go straight into the question and answer session and that Nipper would be on the floor with the roving mike for those asking questions.

The session went ok and then Roberto sat at the top table for anyone interested in photos with him, but surprisingly there were not too many.

Roberto was probably in the function only about two and a half hours and it was a much more relaxed atmosphere than any of the previous shows with no hassle for photos or even autographs. The audience were mainly working class and Roberto appeared to be a lot more comfortable here.

After the show Gra asked if we would be interested in going to a night club with him. I asked Roberto and Tony and because of the time we had on our hands he said no problem.

At the club entrance the doorman was none other than the former British light middle-weight champion Chris Pyatt. An amateur club friend of mine, Graeme Ahmed, who also had a decent career in the professional ranks had been doing quite well until he ran into Chris Pyatt at London when he was stopped in two rounds. Although Graeme had also fought Nigel Benn and other capable names he still insisted that Chris Pyatt was the hardest hitter he had come up against.

Chris was the classic example of one of those rare talented boxers who hit his peak at a weight below the weight he ended up campaigning at on the world scene. Pyatt spent a good few years winning but treading water domestically until he hitched up a bit late in the day with a manager who could move him, albeit at the wrong weight division.

At least Pyatt did win the WBO middleweight title even if he was past his best when the opportunity finally came round. He lost it to Steve Collins before he could really cash in, and what a pity he was the wrong side of 30 when his chance came. It should have come when he won the European title in one round seven years earlier but professional boxing is all about getting the right fights at the right time.

Chris welcomed us all into the club and posed for a couple of photos with us, and then showed us downstairs to the club dance floor. Roberto enjoyed watching the dancers in their skimpy outfits, and appeared very relaxed here.

Word must have got round that Roberto was in the club as a lot of gents who had been to a black-tie boxing dinner event came in and started asking for photos and autographs. I let Gra know that Tony and Roberto were not happy about this, as why should these guys get all of this for free when others at Gra's function had paid for it? So we put a stop on them and then Roberto asked to leave.

We all piled into the limousine outside and Roberto as usual asked for some food. Gra said that everywhere was closed now but there was a takeaway on the way back to the lodge. So we pulled up outside Marios, which was a kind of fast food Italian takeaway. We all ordered and there were a few seats inside so Roberto and Tony and I ate our food inside and the limousine just waited on us outside the main doors. I'll bet that would be the first time that Marios had had a boxing legend eating inside, with an awaiting limousine outside its doors.

Gra arranged to pick us up the following morning to take us across to Birmingham airport for our flight up to Glasgow.

It was only a short flight to Glasgow where promoter Norrie Sweeny and his pal met us at the airport. Norrie was a short guy, early fifties, who had had his heart set on featuring Roberto in Scotland for some time and was helped with his promotion by some of the amateur clubs.

We were driven to Glasgow's Marriott hotel, which was really plush. I asked Norrie to come to my room with the dollars when he could. Norrie had made a slight mistake with the dollar exchange and was a few hundred short. I explained this to him, and he agreed and we took a short walk to an exchange centre where he made up the amount.

Norrie, Tony and I took a walk into the main shopping area for a look around. Tony bought a few Scottish dolls to take back to Miami. Norrie said his dinner was due to start at 7pm and that Tony and I would sit for the dinner and Roberto would come down afterwards.

At the dinner table I sat next to a guy who said he was Ken Buchanan's new agent. He informed me that he was staging a dinner next month for Ken, and Sugar Ray Leonard was attending, I had not heard anything of this so had my doubts about it. Tony let me know that Roberto was not feeling too well and might be going down with some kind of bug. I thought to myself that's all we need for him to take bad, especially when we still had two shows left to do.

Roberto came into the hall to some piped music and someone had put a pair of boxing gloves on him so he shadow boxed his way into the room, which had about 300 people in.

The questions started coming from all angles but once again none that I had not heard before, and none that were targeted towards Roberto not giving Ken a rematch which I thought there would have been.

Norrie had arranged for the photo shoot to be in a room which was quite a walk from the main function room and he also had his own photos for sale there. So after the question and answer session I accompanied Roberto over to the room where he sat at a table and fans were brought in a table at a time.

Tony Gonzalez then pulled off a sting that was a little below the belt. He arranged himself at a table which was positioned on the way to the photo shoot room with piles of his own photos of Roberto and started to sell then to fans before they entered the room. This was of course unknown to Norrie who was inside the room himself.

Tony then had the front to ask me to sit with the remaining photos whilst he went to the top table to try and auction some more of his posters.

I only did this for no longer than a few minutes, as I did not agree with this tact, and Norrie later commented on it to me but by then it was too late – Tony had made his money on them.

The function appeared to do quite well with the auction of a Celtic football shirt bringing in over £1000, and a signed pair of boxing shorts by Roberto bringing £700.

The following morning I was informed that someone had stolen the signed Celtic shirt, which had been left unattended for a short while... not the best thing to do in Glasgow.

The following morning, which was the Saturday, I booked our taxi for 11.30am to take us to Glasgow train station which was only a five minute run and our train to Newcastle was due to leave at 12 midday. I informed Tony of this... but at 11.45 I went to the room for Roberto and he was still getting dressed; he had no track of time whatsoever. Luckily we hit no traffic and only just caught the train.

The train journey was only two hours to Newcastle and

Roberto sat with his headphones on as usual and sang away to himself.

I had previously contacted Mark Hasson of the Newcastle United Football Club to enquire if the club would be interested in parading Roberto onto the pitch. Mark replied to me and said that he had spoken to the relevant people and that they would be delighted to show Roberto to the fans.

At their home ground St James' Park Newcastle United would guarantee to put in 52,000 supporters no matter who they were playing – they had fanatical support. I thought that this would be a good idea, and it would also give Roberto a buzz being introduced to a crowd of that size.

I had spoken with Tony about this a few times whilst on the tour and he appeared fine with it and relayed the idea obviously in Spanish to Roberto, who also seemed ok with it.

So whilst on the train journey to Newcastle Mark was in contact with me and let me know that they would introduce Roberto before the match began at 3pm. I informed him that we were due into Newcastle at around 2.20pm and maybe they could have us picked up and driven to the ground, which was only a short distance away from the train station. Mark kept ringing me back asking our position on the journey, but then asked if we could make our own way to the ground. I honestly thought that the least they could do was pick us up, being a multi-million pound organisation.

I tried whilst on the train to ask for some assistance at Newcastle with our luggage and the staff said that there would be porters awaiting us on the station.

We arrived at Newcastle about 2.25pm and I was still in constant contact with Mark Hasson.

The porters who were supposedly helping us with our luggage were nowhere to be seen so we struggled with it to the station exit, and hopefully would pick up a cab straight away.

This is when I was reminded that it was Great North Run weekend and, unbeknown to me, there was a junior Great North Run on the Saturday followed by the main event on the Sunday.

Because of this the Newcastle City centre road network was completely jammed. The queue for taxis was about 100 yards long, so I knew there was no way we were going to get there before kick-off time. Roberto asked were our transport was. But all I could say was that it was on its way. I tried to contact my brother Bryan who was always very supportive in a crisis, but he told me that one of his wife's family had just spent over two hours trying to drive through Newcastle centre.

We were half way down the queue now and Roberto and Tony were getting impatient, asking what was happening, but I had already explained to them about the Great North Run weekend, and there was little we could do about it.

The time was now about 3.15pm and the match had obviously kicked off. Mark called again asking where we were. and said he would now introduce Roberto at half time. The queue seemed to take forever to go down and there was no way we could walk it with all of our luggage, as at every show Roberto was always presented with some framed picture or other present that added to the amount we had to carry.

We eventually came to near the front of the queue, and there was a student who spoke with a Yorkshire accent on his own when a large black cab pulled in. I asked the student if he would not mind us sharing his cab due to us being in a mad hurry, to which he said no problem as he was travelling to Byker and said he could drop us off first.

The Asian cab driver pulled away but when I told him where we were going he said it would take at least 20 minutes to travel there due to traffic chaos. He was right: we were moving but only just and I could notice Roberto becoming impatient.

Mark called me again and I passed my phone to the driver who informed him where we were and Mark told him where he could park at the football ground.

Eventually we arrived at the ground and an elderly steward took a look into the cab, obviously recognised Roberto and waved us into a small car parking area. I jumped out and a tall guy came over and introduced himself as Mark Hasson. We shook hands and then the unbelievable happened.

I shouted to Roberto and Tony to get out of the cab. Tony spoke to Roberto and he then turned to me and said Roberto wanted to go straight to the hotel. I said we had agreed to come to the football ground and it would not take long, maybe only 15 minutes. Again Tony related this to Roberto but once again he just sat and mumbled in Spanish that he wanted to go straight to the hotel. It was at a time like this that I wished I understood Spanish. The poor student who was jammed in the middle of Tony and Roberto did not know what was happening and only wanted to get to his own destination. I went around to the side of the cab where Roberto was sitting and said to him that he had agreed with me to come here so why was had he changed his mind? He just looked at me and then started saying in broken English that it was too long and he was tired and hungry and only wanted to go to the hotel, and would come back here later.

This really annoyed me, but Mark who had witnessed everything just said not to worry, that he would make an announcement to the 50,000 fans that Roberto was stuck in traffic and would not now be making an appearance, when he was actually only yards away. It was then that I recalled Roberto's elderly manager Carlos Eleta in Panama telling me that "Roberto would only do what he wanted to do".

I climbed back into the cab really disappointed at what had happened. The cab driver and the student were not too happy after driving to the ground in traffic chaos all to come to nothing. The driver said that he would now have to drop the student off at Byker, which was at the East End of Newcastle and about a ten minute drive on a normal day. So I was that mad I thought the quickest way now to get to South Shields where we were staying would be on the underground Metro system, so as we were near the Haymarket metro station I asked the driver to drop us off and paid extra money to the student to cover his fare.

At Haymarket I explained to Tony that this was the only option we had for travelling due to the chaos he had witnessed. So we put our entire luggage into the lift which took us to the platform for South Shields. We only had to wait a couple of minutes for a metro when I got a call from Bryan asking where we were. He said that he would drive to Heworth which was half way, and pick us up there.

On the metro, which was packed but still the quickest form of transport out of the city, Tony said that we could not travel too far carrying all of our luggage; I let him know that we were getting picked up at the next station which was only minutes away.

At Heworth we took the lift to the concourse and Bryan pulled over in my jeep. He climbed out and gave me the keys saying that he was going to jump on the metro himself as he was going into the city. I thanked him and jammed all of our luggage in and drove towards South Shields.

On the way Roberto noticed a Burger King sign and as usual said he was hungry. Tony asked if we could pull in there and have something to eat.

Inside the Burger King I bumped into one of our club former heavyweight boxers Mark Walker who recognised me with Duran and asked if it really was him? Roberto and Tony had their burger meals and there was now obvious tension between us brought about by Roberto's refusal to make an appearance at the game. I honestly felt like just leaving them there but knew I had my own show organised for tonight and still had to take them to Birmingham on the Sunday.

Anyway we had to get on with it so I drove to 'Tuckers Inn' at South Shields and hoped they would be ok with it, as it was only a guesthouse.

Paul Redfern met us at the reception area, which looked quite plush now since my last visit, and I introduced him to Roberto and Tony. Paul showed them to their rooms, which were also fine, and I let them know that I would pick them up later to take them to the show at Sunderland. Paul gave me his mobile number to keep in touch if any problems arose.

I drove home to meet my wife Linda who was a great help at functions along with the Raffle girls Vivienne, Gillian and Paula.

Linda informed me that everything was ok over at the Stadium of Light and there was no need to worry about anything as she had been across earlier in the day to set things up. If Linda said it was fine I knew it would be as she was very fussy.

I rang Paul Redfern who let me know that if need be he and his wife Karen would bring Roberto and Tony over to the function later on the night after the dinner. This would save me a drive back over to South Shields, which could have caused problems due to traffic or whatever, so I agreed for Paul to do this.

We picked Vivienne up on the way and arrived at the function room about an hour before the start time, which was usual for us, as I liked to get things right without any hiccups. The staff at the Stadium of Light were very helpful and professional. Martin Emmerson, whom I had contacted to MC the function, turned up and introduced himself. Martin had previously worked for North East press but was now with Radio Newcastle and had an excellent voice for presentations, I always liked to put it down in black and white for MCs so I handed Martin a few notes, which we ran through together.

On the top table I had invited Mick Worrall, who was the new sports editor for my local paper, the South Shields Gazette, local area former top amateur and professional Graeme Ahmed who was a massive Roberto Duran fan, and also Stuart Rich who was a pal from the Sunderland area whom I had boxed during my own amateur career and who always booked a full table at my shows – so I thought it a nice gesture to have him on the top table.

The audience started arriving, and Martin Emmerson got under way with the introductions and was very impressive. Martin was informed by someone that I had beaten Stu Rich who was sitting next to me, on a stoppage several years ago, which I would have preferred him not to mention and made me wonder who had informed him. He introduced sports editor Mick Worrall, and recalled the time when he was on his works experience at the office where Mick was employed. Mick was a little doubtful about sitting on the top table when I had put the offer to him, as his boss had booked a floor table for his staff, but eventually Mick agreed and I suppose he had the pleasure of looking down at his boss for once.

I received a call from Paul Redfern to say that they had arrived and I already had a waiting room set up for them until we were ready. Once in the room Roberto as usual requested some food so I had four meals brought to them so that Tony, Karen and Paul could also eat.

I thought it might give it a little edge if I brought Roberto in to a fanfare and also a nice young girl to carry the Panamanian flag in front of him. I had a task getting hold of a Panamanian flag as I was informed it is not commonly requested, but eventually a local dealer sent one to me. I asked Graeme Ahmed who had a stunning 15 year old daughter Carly if she would do the honours and walk Roberto in, to which he was only too happy to oblige, and the entrance went as planned.

Roberto received a great reception from the audience and handled the question and answer session well. He had the audience laughing when someone asked if it was true that whilst in his youth he used to mug sailors to help support his family at Panama. With a cheeky grin he replied, "No it was Miami."

The questions dried up as usual after about 30 minutes and I escorted Roberto straight over to a table where the photo session was going to take place. Jimmy Patterson, our photographer, was all set up but there was no security whatsoever and we had been previously promised this by Barbara Bewick who was not in attendance at the function. This was quite common when organising evening functions as, although you agreed things with staff during the day, when it came to function time they had all gone home and sometimes forgot to inform whoever was there at night about requirements. My wife Linda knew exactly how to go on with this type of session and took over until things settled down to stop queue jumping and those taking longer than necessary with photos and autographs.

I asked Roberto if he wanted to go to a club or anywhere after the function but he said he would rather not as he was getting a little tired with all of the travelling.

Paul and Karen drove Roberto and Tony back to their 'Tuckers Inn' guest house and I spent the night at home, and dropped off a lot of the unnecessary luggage I had been carrying and just packed a bag for the last show at Telford.

With it being the morning of the Great North Run I had to catch an early Metro train to South Shields and then had a ten-minute walk to Tuckers Inn.

I sat chatting with Karen and Paul, who were both very hospitable, until Roberto and Tony arose. Due to the Great North Run all of the roads to Newcastle were closed and although Paul said he would take us through the Tyne Tunnel to Newcastle I said that I did not want to take that risk and we would take the metro system which would be much quicker and drop us right off at Newcastle's Central Station to catch our connecting train to Birmingham. Paul agreed with me so when Roberto and Tony eventually arose Paul drove us the short ride to South Shields metro station which was not as busy as I had expected and we all obtained seats without any problem.

At Newcastle Station Roberto once again gave his usual cry of "I Hungry" so I bought them a couple of burgers each whilst we awaited the train to Birmingham.

I had acquired first class tickets for this journey which was only a little extra when purchased well in advance and I thought it a safer idea with the Great North Run being on, and maybe people travelling back home.

The club class carriage was excellent with only a handful of people in it, and we had plenty of room.

Roberto sat opposite Tony and I sat at the table behind them. Roberto immediately put on his music system and started his shouting and screaming antics, which were really loud. Tony said to me that he was happy now because he knew the tour was nearly over and it would not be long before he was going home to Panama.

An elderly lady was sitting across from me and she started giving Roberto strange looks when he was singing out loud in Spanish and was obviously not amused by it all. Tony feel asleep and every now and again Roberto would roll small pieces of paper up into a ball and chuck them at Tony and scream out loud something in Spanish, much to the disgust of the elderly lady across from me.

This went on for most of the nearly three hour journey, and the lady then asked me where the train stewards were. The lady was not happy about the antics of Roberto and wanted to report him. I said to her that he was fine and just having a little bit of fun as he was on his way home to Panama. Roberto stopped his singing but then decided to play some bongo drum tunes on his table. Having seen him play these in Panama, even on the train table I could make out a steady rhythm beat.

The elderly lady muttered something to me and stood up and then stormed out of the carriage. I only hoped she had not gone for the stewards, as the last thing I wanted was for some stewards to come along and try and throw us off the train, but she must have either moved carriages or got off the train as that was the last I saw of her.

On arrival at Birmingham Eric Ragonesi and his brother met us and took our luggage to his huge Range Rover. Eric's brother ran a jewellery shop in Birmingham's jewellery quarter and as we had to pass this way to Telford Eric asked if we would like a look at the shop premises, to which Roberto agreed.

The premises were quite large with security cameras all around it. Eric's brother went into the back shop and brought a bag full of gold watches, rings and other items for us to look at. Roberto was very interested in the gold and informed us he had spent a little time in his youth working with gold, and Tony confirmed this but could not give us too many details about it.

As we were looking at different items I noticed Roberto signing his name on the back of anything that was lying about on the counter. He had a habit of doing this wherever he went and I collected several items that he had done small drawings on. On a tablecloth at the Stadium of Light he had done several small drawings of fish and a matchstick drawing of Tony. He also signed the Panamanian flag for me 'Roberto Duran' 'Manos de

Piedra' which is Spanish for 'hands of stone'.

We left the jewellery quarter and Eric took us to the small hotel where we dropped our luggage off and then took a stroll out for something to eat. There were not too many places open as it was about 5pm on a Sunday but we eventually found a small Kebab place where Eric bought us some food.

Back at the hotel Joe Pyle rang me and asked if he could speak to Tony. I gave Tony a call to come to my room and returned the call for him to speak to Joe regarding the put up boxing bout that he was trying to organise. Tony asked if I would contact Ken Purchase for him as he was owed some money from him and also to try and get hold of Glyn Rhodes again. I did this while Tony was there but there was no reply from either of them, but I let him know both were genuine guys and anything that they owed him he would eventually get from them.

Tony then said that, as they had to be at London's Heathrow airport at 8am on the Monday morning for their 11am flight to Miami, they would like to leave immediately after the show and book into a hotel at Heathrow. I suggested that it would be better for us to stay the night at the Telford hotel where Eric had booked us into and just leave about 6am the following morning, but he insisted on leaving after the show.

This meant that apart from me having to provide a taxi fare to London, Tony would also require me to book into a hotel at Heathrow which I knew from previous experience would cost a fortune and you would also have a game on getting booked into one now, so there was no way I was going to agree and have to pay for this.

When we agreed the contracts I made sure that I was only responsible for providing overnight accommodation for five nights. I had missed this small but very important clause out on our first contract agreement but in reality if left out this meant that they could have stayed for any amount of nights and I had to provide accommodation for them, so this time I made sure I had the contract with me and ready to produce it if Tony tried to ask me to pay for their stay at Heathrow.

Eric came to pick us up at the hotel and take us to his club, which was a nightclub called Club 42. I thought it was going to be jam-packed but there were probably only about a hundred people in. A DJ gave Roberto a huge entrance and we were taken over to a small corner of the room which was cordoned off. The DJ had previously collected questions to be put to Roberto written down on paper from the punters. Initially those who had written the questions down were called to the DJ stand to use the mike but this was taking far too long so I suggested to the DJ that he should just ask all of the questions himself and this was much better as some could not handle using a mike.

After this we all went back to the cordoned off area and fans were allowed to queue for photos and autographs. Eric had Roberto sign a few gloves and pictures that he was going to auction off and took his shirt off to square up with Roberto and had a bit of fun with him and a press photo.

The next thing I knew there were about six topless models arrived from the Sunday Sport newspaper. Eric had obviously set this up and Roberto appeared to be quite at home with them as they posed for photos with him and a few asked him to sign their upper body parts. They then made themselves available for dances with whoever was willing to pay for them.

I let Eric know that Roberto and Tony had now decided that they wanted to leave straight after the show and asked him if he could organise a taxi ride to Heathrow for us; he said that this would be no problem.

We packed our luggage and took the taxi ride to Heathrow which was driven by one of the club door staff. After about an hour's drive we stopped at a service station and Roberto and Tony used the toilets and picked up a few bags of sweets and chocolate in the shop. I asked the driver what time we would arrive at Heathrow. He reckoned about 3am.

Sure enough we arrived at just a little before 3am and it was then that Tony said to me, "What hotel have you booked us into?" I said that I had not booked into any because I was not too sure what his intentions were and how the night would go at

Club 42, but apart from that trying to get through to book into hotels at Heathrow is hard at any time, so it would probably be better just to turn up and hope for the best.

I then reminded Tony that because I had covered the cost of accommodation for the five nights as per our contract and we were into our seventh night that he would have to pay the hotel bill if they decided to stay at one for the few hours that were remaining before their check in time of 8am. Tony replied this was not the case as he had made out the contract and I was responsible for providing accommodation from when they arrived until they left the UK. I said that this was not the case in the contract.

The driver went around in circles a few times trying to get to a hotel that we could see on the outskirts of the airport but had a job getting to by road. When we eventually got to the reception desk, I checked the room costs which were £175 per night, so if Tony thought that I was going to fork out £350 for him and Roberto to spend a few hours, he had better think again.

Tony then rang the bell for reception and whilst we were waiting I asked him to take a look at the contract, which I had ready and which clearly stated that I, the promoter, provided overnight accommodation for five nights. Tony then said that Joe Pyle had paid for one night to which I agreed but this was our seventh night and the other five had been provided by me by way of the individual promoters. Tony then said that "if that was the way I wanted it well OK and he was not going to argue with me".

I replied that he should have taken my advice and stayed at the Telford hotel where everything was provided and paid for.

As it was now approaching 4.00am I suggested to him that we drive across to Terminal 3 which was where they were flying out from and if need be they could get a couple of hours' sleep on the seating areas, which was what I was going to do at Terminal 1 before my flight back to Newcastle.

The thought then came across my mind that if Roberto had spent a lot of his youth sleeping on the streets of Panama, a couple of hours sleeping in the warm and comfort of Heathrow would be nothing to him, and surely on his travels around the world during his career he and Tony would have experienced this at many airports.

The driver pulled up at Terminal 3 and we all lifted our luggage out of the back. Roberto came over to me and gave me a big hug and said thank you and goodbye. Tony just shook my hand and said nothing. We then made our own ways to the different Terminal entrances.

Before my journey back to Newcastle I received a call from Glyn Rhodes asking how things had gone and letting me know that he had had several calls from unsatisfied customers about Roberto leaving his function early, and because of it he would not be welcome back in Sheffield again. Glyn also said that regarding the payment to Tony for posters or photos he had nothing to do with them, but would try and chase them up, as to who had received the money for them.

I received a similar phone call from Ken Purchase, who said that although his show went ok, Tony Gonzalez had been far too demanding for money for items signed by Roberto and also very doubtful if he would be welcome back.

When I arrived back home to Newcastle it was a huge relief that the tour was over. This time it was not as enjoyable as the first tour, and Tony was a lot more demanding financially. Roberto was the same Roberto, always laughing and carrying on, always hungry and doing as he wanted to do. It was a pity it ended on a sour note with Tony as I had made a lot of money for them, organising shows over a two year period.

I thought it would be a long time before Roberto would be back at any shows in the UK as we had covered virtually everywhere, and those who wanted to would have seen him; nevertheless I would make him more than welcome if he ever made a visit to the UK again.

It was now time to move on and look at other boxing celebrities who may be worthwhile featuring, as I felt that after handling Duran, I could handle anybody.

After a long time of trying, I followed the Duran tours by setting up a tour and travelling with World boxing legend Thomas 'The Hitman' Hearns and his trainer Emanuel Steward and then tours with the one and only Sugar Ray Leonard.

ROY SHAW, MARTYN AND ROBERTO DURAN, LONDON, 2003

JOE PYLE SNR, ROY SHAW, ROBERTO DURAN & FREDDIE FOREMAN, LONDON UNDERWORLD FIGURES, 2003

ROBERTO & MARTYN WITH JOE PYLE JNR AND HIS BOYS, LONDON, 2003

DURAN MEETING BRITISH CHAMPIONS AT SHEFFIELD, 2003

MARTYN AND TONY SIBSON, LEICESTER, 2003

MARTYN WITH ERIC RAGONESI AND PALS, 2003

THOMAS HEARNS AND EMANUEL STEWARD TOUR 2004

Thomas Hearns was born on 18th October 1958 in Memphis, Tennessee. His mother moved the family to Detroit for better prospects when he was only five and it was there he took up boxing as a ten year old. Thomas eventually joined the famous Kronk Amateur boxing gym to be trained by the legendary Emanuel 'Manny' Steward. Tommy won 147 out of 155 bouts and decided to turn professional during 1977 aged 19. As a professional he ran up a record of 28 fights with 17 KOs before challenging for his first world title at welterweight against the legendary Mexican Pipino Cuevas. Hearns ended Cuevas's four year reign by way of a second round KO. It was then that the fight against Sugar Ray Leonard was made to unify the welterweight tiles. With Hearns unbeaten after 32 fights with 30 KOs behind him and Leonard at 30 fights with only one defeat against Roberto Duran, this was going to be one of the biggest fights in boxing history. Hearns built up a big lead after 12 rounds and then Leonard with his left eye nearly closed was told by his corner man Angelo Dundee that

"He was blowing it". Leonard then went after Hearns looking for the knock out and hurt him with several hard shots that forced the referee to give Tommy a count of eight. The fourteenth round saw Leonard start where he had finished and threw a barrage of hard punches to the head and body of Tommy, who, although trying to fight back, was saved by the referee after one minute and 45 seconds of the round. Tommy then moved up to Junior middleweight to challenge Puerto Rican legend Wilfredo Benitez for the WBC title and won a points decision after 15 rounds of supreme skilful boxing. Roberto Duran challenged for Tommy's title on 15th June 1984 and was KO'd midway into the second round after being caught by a stunning right hand punch. Tommy then moved up to middleweight to challenge Marvelous Marvin Hagler for the undisputed crown and after two rounds of blistering action Tommy was KO'd midway through the third round. When he defeated Virgil Hill on 3rd June 1991 to win the WBA Light Heavyweight title Tommy Hearns went into the history books by becoming the first man to win four titles in four different weight divisions. His career ended with an impressive record of 60 fights, five losses and one draw. Tommy scored 48 KOs.

THE CONTACT

I was contacted during October 2003 by a local football agent by the name of Carl Dunn from the South Shields area regarding featuring the legendary Thomas 'Hit Man' Hearns and his well respected trainer Emanuel 'Manny' Steward over in the UK. Carl was handling affairs for the Sunderland boxer David Dolan who boxed out of the Plains Farm ABC and had recently won the Gold Medal at the Commonwealth Games in Canada.

Carl asked me to meet him at his office unit down at the Tedco business park at Jarrow. I met him along with David Dolan whom I already knew from my amateur connections. Carl said that he and David had been over to Detroit to take a look at Emanuel Steward's set up over there with a view to David turning professional and that he wanted to bring Manny over here and stage a few sporting dinners with one of them being at Newcastle. I was a little taken aback at first, as I was the only one staging sporting dinners featuring boxers at that time but sat and listened to what he had to say.

Carl told me the fee he was paying and then asked if I would help with ticket sales at Newcastle and that he had nothing to do with the other shows which were going to be in Scotland and Teesside. I found this set up strange and asked Carl if he had a contract in place as I had been used to working to contracts when featuring big names from the USA. He showed me one piece of paper with a small note on saying that Manny and Tommy had agreed to appear on set dates. I asked if that was all he had and he said it was. This again I found strange as the contracts I had dealt with were usually about four pages long with detailed descriptions of what the guests would do, and travel and accommodation etc, and a detailed note on fees. Carl let me know that he was a football agent but was also handling a few things for David.

I said I would consider it and would call him later that day. On returning home I had a think about it but because of no contract in place and because of the time of year being December I knew I would have a job selling it, so gave Carl a ring and rejected his offer, but said I would take it on at Newcastle for a reduced fee; however, Carl said the fee had already been agreed upon.

Later that month I received an international call and it was from Emanuel Steward himself asking if I was interested in staging any dinners featuring him. I did tell him that it was a bad time of year now but would set something up in the future so long as he brought Tommy Hearns with him. Manny said Tommy did not talk that well now and that it would be better if he came by himself. I said I would keep in touch, but knew that I would not be able to sell Manny by himself.

I then received a call from a friend during November 2003 who had booked to see Tommy Hearns and Manny at Newcastle to say that the show had been cancelled along with other UK dates and asked if I knew anything about it? I did tell him about Carl and said that December was a bad time of year for selling shows due to being too close to Xmas.

It was at this time I was dealing with Bjorn Rebney, agent for Sugar Ray Leonard and was trying to set a tour up for Ray in the UK in 2004. The tour ran into problems due to Ray's break up with Rebney over The Contender programme.

It was then I thought about the call from Manny Steward and thought rather than cancel everything why not try and put Manny and Tommy Hearns on, in place of Ray Leonard.

I therefore contacted Manny and without mentioning anything about Ray Leonard I asked if he was still interested in coming to the UK, but insisted that he would have to bring Tommy Hearns with him. Manny said he would love to come over and immediately started telling me some great tales from behind the scenes about Tommy and some of his fights and also Alexis Arguello and Aaron Pryor. I then started to think about how much this phone call was costing me and suggested to Manny that he could keep all these tales for when he comes over.

So I then put a contract together and faxed it over to him to look at. After a week went by I contacted his office secretary

Lannie and asked if Manny was around. Lannie said that she had misplaced the contract I had sent and asked if I could fax it over again. I did this, but then had the first hint of unprofessionalism.

Manny was hired by a lot of top world champions and travelled the globe to major title fights, so he was quite hard to nail down. Nevertheless I made contact with him and asked if things were ok with the contract and he said no problem, so I asked if he and Tommy could sign the contract and return it to me to enable me to put the tour together. This took a little time but sure enough the contract was faxed back across signed by both Thomas Hearns and Emanuel Steward.

I did make sure that I did not put any set amount of dates within the contract until I was in touch with the other promoters.

On contacting the other promoters who had previously booked Sugar Ray, only one of them, Chris Sanigar, agreed to take on Hearns and Steward. I was a little shocked at this as it was at a reduced fee to Ray Leonard's, but then thought about how they'd been let down with the Leonard tour and this must have discouraged them from taking anything else on.

I then contacted Kevin Sanders from Peterborough who had featured Duran and he said he was very interested in featuring Hearns and Steward. Ken Purchase from Telford also contacted me to let me know of his interest; Ken had also featured Roberto Duran and staged big shows with a big memorabilia auction filling a major part of his functions. So this gave a definite four shows, so I confirmed with Manny and hinted there could possibly be more.

Glyn Rhodes from Sheffield had reserved a date for the Tuesday for Leonard, and he asked me to hold the date for him for Hearns, but said he was having a few problems with his sponsor. I could not understand why sponsorship came into it as I personally just worked off ticket sales to make it pay, but I suppose each Promoter had their own ways of making the event financially worthwhile.

I was quite confident about Glyn putting a show on but after giving him more than enough time he eventually left a message on my answer machine saying he was pulling out. So this meant I still had two nights free with Manny and Tommy.

A guy from London called Lee Short contacted me and said he was a partner and pal of Charlie Magri, the former world flyweight champion, and he would be interested in featuring any big names in the London area. I informed him about Tommy and Manny coming over and he said he was very interested, so I forwarded him a contract to look at. Later that week he said he would like to go for it and booked the Saturday night in London; this was convenient as they would need to be in London for their flight back to the States.

So this made up five shows which was ideal, and would give them one free night when I would have to look after them. Staging tours was difficult in the way that ideally you would start off at either the top of the country and work your way down or vice versa, but the problem was that promoters had their set nights when staging shows, so you had to work the tour to suit them.

As it happened I had booked the tour to start at Newcastle on Saturday 9th October and finish at London on the 16th with their departure booked for the 17th.

A new promoter contacted me from the Preston area by the name of Adrian Worth whom I had never heard of. He said he would like to feature Tommy there on the Monday 11th. I told him the fee, sent the contract and he returned it signed within the week. He sounded very young but came across ok and said he had been involved in the amateurs and was a friend of Michael Jennings who boxed on a lot of the Ricky Hatton fight bills in Manchester.

Adrian later contacted me to say that he could not get the venue on the Monday but could do it on the Sunday, to which I said was fine by me. I personally found Sundays were always a bad night for functions as most people had work the following day and it was still a day when not a lot happened, although some of the big football matches were still played, but I was not going to stop him as it was another date booked and would save me having to look after them for that night.

So with the Saturday, Sunday, Wednesday Thursday, Friday and Saturday booked that was six shows, which was ideal but still meant I had to look after them on the Monday and Tuesday.

Although I would have worked on something to fill those nights I decided to take a look at contacting another few promoters and see if they were interested. One of them was a guy called Lee Maloney from the Liverpool area who staged professional boxing at the Everton sports centre. I gave Lee a call and he came across as a nice guy and said he would have a chat with his partner and get back to me.

I came home from a Sunday night out for a few beers and my wife Linda said she had been speaking to a lovely guy on the phone from Belfast who was interested in bringing Tommy and Manny over there, and he was going to ring back at midnight.

Sure to his word Damian McCann called me at midnight. Damian ran the Kronk amateur gym in Belfast and had been in touch with Emanuel Steward over the past few years, first of all to allow them to use his name for their gym, and more recently over the interest Manny had in Ireland's only boxer in the Athens Olympics, Andy Lee.

Damian had obviously heard about Manny coming over to England and said wouldn't it be great if he could come over to Belfast and officially open their gym?

I informed Damian that Manny was coming with Tommy Hearns and that there was a fee for their appearance at the functions, but nevertheless I said I would contact Manny and put the proposal to him. Damian came across as a genuine guy and had certainly charmed Linda when he told her he was RC and had four daughters, and a wife who was also called Linda.

I then received a call from Lee Maloney saying that although it was short notice he was willing to give it a go and feature Tommy and Manny in Liverpool on the Tuesday the 12th October at the famous Adelphi Hotel. So this would give them seven shows with the possibility of a visit to Belfast.

I contacted Manny about the visit to Belfast and he said it would not be a problem, why not?

So I informed Damian about this and said the only available day we could come was on the Monday, and so long as he would pay our travel expenses and accommodation it would be ok, provided there were no paying customers and no organised signing sessions. Damian said he would get back to me with confirmation.

So things were now in place, with every night covered for what would be a hectic week of travelling from Newcastle to Preston then down to Manchester airport to fly to Belfast then back across to Manchester to travel to Liverpool then on to Telford across to Peterborough back over to Bristol and then over to London for the last show and a departure on the 17th October.

One of the promoters said that he would not sign a contract, nor would he make a deposit which was a condition of the contract. This particular promoter was a man of his word and always stuck to his agreement.

I noticed in the boxing news some of the promoters were advertising the function but others were not. The only two that I had not dealt with were Adrian Worth from Preston and Lee Maloney from Liverpool, so I decided I had to do a little homework on them, to make sure they were genuine, as one has to do in this game.

Lee Maloney was a professional boxing promoter from the Liverpool area, which was an area I had not dealt with but did have a contact there who informed me that although there were a lot of dodgy customers in the Liverpool area Lee Maloney was clean and had a good name.

Adrian Worth had been a decent amateur himself and said he had been to the Durham College of Excellence. I contacted a guy from his area and he said Adrian was a genuine lad and helped out at an Amateur club.

I contacted Adrian about his deposit which had not come through. He said that he would be in touch. Time went by so I had to contact him again and asked what venue he was using; he informed me about a hotel on the M6 motorway which was very plush. I was under the impression, because he had mentioned he was a friend of Michael Jennings and Ricky Hatton, that all of Hatton's followers would be helping him out. After a while I made contact with the hotel and they said it was unconfirmed. So I made contact with Adrian again and he said he had now changed the venue. This all sounded a little strange but he did sound very genuine and I gave him more time for his deposit, and let him know that you had to be certain when staging an event like this as you cannot afford to let anyone down. I contacted the new venue which was a council civic hall and they gave me the contact number of Adrian's partner, a guy called Joe.

I had difficulty making contact with Joe but when I eventually did get through to him he said he had just come out of hospital with gallstone trouble, and that Adrian had been handling things. Time was getting on now with about six weeks to go to their show and I had never seen it advertised, there was no deposit paid and it was hard to make contact with them at times.

I eventually made contact with Adrian and said that I would personally advertise the event in Boxing News for him, as time was getting on. He said that Joe had his own building business and would be sending the deposit soon, and that they were definitely going ahead with the function.

Damian McCann sent confirmation of the visit to Belfast and sent our flight tickets the following day. Damian was very switched on and organised, which I suppose was easy when you were having two of the biggest names in boxing in your home town for free.

There were just a few loose ends to tidy up now and then organise travel arrangements to get from venue to venue. I usually organised this by way of having the show promoter pick us up from the previous night's show and take us to their venue. This way it was easier as they knew their way around their areas and it also gave them the chance to meet their guests beforehand, and also saved me on the expenses. So the tour was now set to start at Newcastle on October 9th.

When I returned home from work on Friday 8th October Linda

said I had to ring Manny's secretary Lannie to speak to Emanuel Steward immediately; panic now set in as this told me something was wrong. I got straight through to Lannie who said that there was a problem with Thomas getting a flight over and that she would put me over onto Manny. Manny came on and said that Thomas was still in Atlanta, Georgia and could not get a flight on time back to Detroit to fly out with Manny. I then felt as though I had been taken for a ride. I said surely he knew about the timing and I said that if Tommy could not come over it was pointless Manny coming on his own. Lannie eventually somehow put me on to to Tommy who mumbled that he had no decent clothes with him and could not make it. I panicked now and told him he had to come to meet his fans who were waiting to see him and I would sort clothes out for him. Tommy sounded drunk but then I had read somewhere that Tommy always slurred his words and he spoke with a deep southern drawl. I begged him for to come over and that he would make a lot of his fans unhappy if he did not come as they were all looking forward to seeing him. He spoke to Lannie and said he did not want to travel without Manny, but Manny had probably already left. Lannie then took the phone and said she would do her best and warned me that Tommy was a snappy dresser and it would cost me to kit him out. I contacted a friend named Jamie who lived just up the street and worked for KLM Airlines and I asked him if he could get a flight for Tommy sorted out from Atlanta to Detroit and then over here. I went up to see Jamie and he was absolutely excellent; he played about on his laptop for ten minutes then said it was sorted and that he had booked Tommy on the next flight out but not with Manny so it was just a case of Tommy getting on the plane at the right time. All I could do now was hope for the best. Jamie contacted me the next morning to say that both seats were taken on the flights but he could not guarantee who was in them for security reasons. This all added a few more grey hairs for me. Manny's flight was due in at 10am via Amsterdam and Tommy on the next flight at about 2pm.

When you are waiting at the Airport for these world boxing

legends to arrive it is a massive worry to think that they will not turn up and you have to relay the news to all of the local fans and the other promoters, so the feeling of doubt you get is indescribable, especially when you have had an earlier problem with flights.

Manny's flight arrived spot on time and I recognised Manny immediately and introduced myself but he did not look too happy and told me that some of his luggage had been lost in transit. I drove Manny down to the Copthorne Hotel. He said he would have to make a few phone calls and then we would go back to the Airport to hopefully pick up Tommy at 2pm.

Manny asked me if I could take him somewhere to pick a mobile phone up and have it decoded as he had a lot of calls to make and take. I took him up to my workplace at the Eldon Square shopping centre and to the Link mobile phone shop to buy a phone and then into the Grainger Market to have his new phone decoded. Manny stopped at a fruit stall and bought a bagful of fruit and carton of strawberries. We then went to the airport to await Tommy's flight which was going to be delayed for 45 mins.

Manny and I just sat in the waiting area and Manny read the local newspapers but he asked why there was no boxing in them, only football. I explained to Manny that boxing was a minority sport over here whereas football was huge. Manny asked about my gym and about the training we did in the amateurs these days; he said that he saw many trainers spending too much time on boxers' training outside of the ropes on hoops and weights and not enough on actual boxing moves and technique inside the ring. He went to the KLM desk and asked if his luggage was on Tommy's flight and was informed that it was. Thank God for that!

Tommy's flight came in 45 minutes late. The unmistakeable Thomas 'Hitman' Hearns came through the doors quite early; he was taller than I expected and also darker. He was dressed in a smart black leather jacket and striped shirt. He looked very tired but shook my hand and then mumbled something to Manny about the flight. I drove them back down to the Copthorne Hotel and sorted Tommy's room out and then brought three of my own suits into his room to show him as I thought he might be a similar size although he looked taller and also broader than me. Tommy looked at the suits, a black one, a beige one and a Prince of Wales check and he said with a smirk on his face "That ain't me, man" so I laughed and said we would have to wait until tomorrow as the shops would be closing in Newcastle as it was after 5pm.

I arranged to meet Tommy and Manny at 9pm to take them to the show and they were spot on time. I drove them up in my car after leaving the dinner at about 8.30 after the meal and set it up so we went in the back door as the comedian was on stage. The comedian Rudi West only did about 15 minutes but I still had to pay him his full asking fee.

Tommy and Manny got a great reception from the audience and the MC Dave Greener went straight out into the audience for the question and answer session. Manny was excellent at this -- having worked for the US TV networks for some time he could talk forever about boxing. Tommy struggled a little at first and found it hard to understand the different accents, but he did eventually open up and shared a few laughable comments with the audience. The photo and autograph session took time, but Tommy signed most things put in front of him although he did take a long time to sign autographs. Tommy pulled me to one side at the finish and asked me how much he was getting for this but I told him he would have to ask Manny as I had done the deal with him. I got the impression that Tommy did not usually do any dinners or talk-ins and that he would not last the week.

We left the hotel and on the way back Manny said he was a little hungry so I pulled into a takeaway near the Centre for Life where I bought them chicken and chips. Tommy and Manny could not believe the number of young girls who were walking the streets with very little clothing on as they were both feeling the cold northern weather. We got back to the Copthorne Hotel after midnight and all turned in after a long and busy day.

The following morning I had a bath then called Tommy and Manny to go for breakfast but they came down far too late and missed it. Tommy asked me to enquire about putting a show together at the Newcastle Arena which he had taken notice of when passing over the Redheugh Bridge.

My brother Bryan met me at Central Station to take my car back home and we then took the train to Carlisle and then to Preston. The Carlisle train was an old slow shuttle which stopped at every station. Tommy sat next to Manny and I sat behind them. Tommy looked crammed into his seat with his knees high up. The next train we caught to Preston was a first class Virgin train which was excellent with plenty of room and much faster. We waited at Preston for a few minutes before Adrian and Joe picked us up in a large jeep. On the way to the hotel I asked Joe if he could take us to some shops where Tommy could pick a couple of suits up. We ended up at a Debenhams store at Preston and Tommy got rigged up with two suits, a suit carrier and a couple of ties, and Manny picked up two shirts. The bill came to £550 and guess who had to pay? We stayed at a Jarvis hotel and after having our rooms sorted Manny, Tommy and I came down for a snack. Tommy mentioned that he had a strong faith and still went to church every Sunday.

We were driven to the show in a Bentley. The show was not very well attended with only about 120 people there. A young guy in the front row was drunk and kept coming up to the front table pestering us, and it was then I saw a different side of Adrian who ended up putting him out. The question and answer session was quite good as they had a very good MC. Later they took Tommy and Manny to a room and started the photo session but had no organised photographer and no security, so I started handling things to help them out and told him to charge £10 for the photos to help him out and keep the queue down as they must have taken a financial hit on the show. We were taken back from the show by an Asian guy called Paul Singh who had a very fast Peugeot and he asked Tommy if he would like to see it motor.

The following morning I sat with Michael Jennings and his

mother who were all really nice people. Michael was doing well in the welterweight professional ranks and boxed on a lot of the Ricky Hatton bills. Mr John Walsh turned up from Bradford again for signings.

Adrian and Steve drove us to Manchester airport for our flight to Belfast. The flight was delayed by an hour. Tommy had one of his new suits on. I showed him my phone which had a game of ten pin bowling on; I showed Tommy how to handle it and he played a couple of games. Our flight eventually came in and as Tommy was trying to put his other new suit amongst his luggage the zip broke on his suit carrier. Tommy struggled to repair it and Manny laughed and said he had told him that the price was too good to be true. Tommy told me his wife's name was Renee and he had two boys and two girls.

I sat next to Tommy on the flight but he looked tired and uncomfortable as the seats were really tight for him and he sat with his head resting on his hand. He asked for cranberry juice but they had none so he just then asked for water. Manny sat across from us and I laughed as Tommy stole one of his sandwiches while he slept. Tommy joked to the air hostess and asked her to pour some hot tea over Manny to wake him. Tommy told me a story about a spider monkey he once had and how he would knock a monkey out that boarded his car. Tommy appeared to be settling down now and we were developing a good friendship between us.

We arrived at Belfast airport and were met by Damian McCann, who was a real down to earth, friendly guy. We went to Damian's house for tea and sandwiches and met his lovely wife Linda and their four daughters. We stayed for about half an hour but I could tell Tommy was not comfortable and wanted to go after a while, so I asked Damian when we were going to the gym. He suggested we go now as the reporters had turned up. It was only a short drive to the Kronk gym which was an old building with a room converted into a gym; it was not very big but had a large ring in place and a few punch-bags around it. There appeared to be hundreds of youngsters there and they kept coming in from all angles. Damian put a couple of them into the ring to spar and the club coach Tony shouted the orders out. As more reporters arrived Damian said he would like Manny to officially open the gym and asked him and Tommy to climb into the ring. TV crews interviewed Manny and Tommy and they posed for photos and signed lots of autographs for the youngsters.

We were then driven to the Belfast Civic Hall which was a beautiful building and we were met by the Mayor. We were given a lovely reception and shown around the building and the Mayor said how proud he was to have us there and we were given tea and biscuits.

Damian and his team then drove us all to a pub where we were given a lovely meal. Tommy sat next to Linda, Damian's wife, who took a few of Tommy's chips. We all laughed when Tommy joked that he never shared his wife, his money or his food. As were waiting on our transport there was a steep bank outside and Tommy jokingly ran up the bank and back down as though he were in training. We all had a good laugh with him and I thought to myself what a smashing guy Tommy was with a great sense of humour.

Back at the hotel which was called the Europa, Tommy and Manny went to bed and I stayed up and had a few drinks with Damian, Tony and Pat. Damian told me that this hotel was the most bombed hotel in Belfast. I suggested he better not let Tommy know!

At breakfast the next morning, another couple of reporters came for interviews with Manny and Tommy. Manny was fine with them but Tommy could not be bothered and you could tell he wanted to be on the move.

Damian drove us to the airport for our flight back to Manchester. I sat next to Tommy and he asked for a blanket and said he was freezing.

We were picked up at Manchester airport and driven to Liverpool Holiday Inn where I met up with the show promoter Lee Maloney. Lee came across as a nice, down to earth guy who also ran a cleaning business and was dabbling with boxing promotions. At the hotel Tommy asked if he could have his suit cleaned as he could smell smoke on it. I then recall Lannie telling me over the phone from Detroit that Tommy had been spoilt. Tommy was very punctual and met at the time I asked. Whilst we were awaiting transport and Manny, Tommy asked me again how much he was getting for these shows. I told him that I had done the deal with Manny and to ask him, but I found it strange that he didn't know.

The function was held at the famous Adelphi hotel and we met up with Lee and Nick from the newspaper that had helped promote the show. The meal seemed to take forever, and one drunken guy near the front was screaming out all the time and Tommy kept asking me what he was saying. Tommy then asked me how much Manny was being paid. I once again said for him to ask Manny. I then pulled Manny quietly to one side and let him know that Tommy was asking about his cut and did not realise that this had not been sorted between them before they left the US. Manny then told me he would sort it out but this made me feel real uneasy.

The show was not that well attended and Lee told me he had taken a financial hit on it. There was very little security and the photo session was disorganised and Tommy got fed up after one hour and asked me to leave with him. Manny told Lee that he should come to one of Martyn's shows to see how it was done; Lee said he would do this and that he would come over to our hotel before we left for Telford to have his gloves signed.

I noticed towards the end of the function Tommy and Manny went over to one side of the hotel foyer area and were talking for a while. Manny then called me over and said he was going to head home tomorrow after discussing a few things with Tommy that Tommy was not happy about – this was obviously over whatever payment they had agreed on. I said to them both that I had four more dinners organised for them both and then angrily pointed to the young barman and explained to them that it would take him all year to earn what they were being paid for one night and explained to them about the average wage in the UK and the massive unemployment figures. I also added how nice it must be to be paid for telling a few stories about something you love and for having your photograph taken and signing autographs.

Manny asked me if he could have a few minutes in private with Tommy. He then called me over and said they had agreed to see out the rest of the tour and we all shook hands. They must have agreed on their individual cuts and that was certainly a weight off my back. Manny asked me to split the payments and asked me to give a set amount to Tommy personally. Thank God!

Lee Maloney turned up after breakfast to have a few pair of gloves signed which Tommy did without any problem.

The next show promoter was Ken Purchase who turned up in a large limousine that was going to take us to Telford near Birmingham. Ken was a large, loud promoter who did things his way and always wanted a little bit extra for his money. Ken asked if Tommy would sign a few things for him whilst travelling in the limousine. Tommy started to do this but struggled after a while and told Ken he would do them at the hotel. The drive to Telford was about two hours, and unless I am sitting facing straight ahead in a limousine I get a headache so I asked Ken If I could move from sitting on the side seats to sit alongside Tommy in the back. Tommy had his eyes closed after a half hour of travel – probably the jet lag and travel starting to kick in.

Ken asked me if Tommy and Manny would do a 15 minute interview with a TV company and he would get them compensated for it. Tommy and Manny agreed but said they would like to get settled in the hotel first. I went to the room with Tommy and he asked if he could have his other suit cleaned, so I contacted Ken Purchase who said he would get it done for him. I had to laugh at Manny as when I was in his room with him Manny would wash his own underwear and socks in the sink and dry them on the heaters. I suppose Manny was used to this after years of travelling on the road with boxers.

The TV guy asked me if Tommy and Manny would come down to a room that they had set up as soon as they were ready. Tommy looked as though he could not be bothered but Manny was very good at working with the media. Manny took over most of the interview but then had a coughing fit halfway through, and then his mobile phone started ringing. I was at the back of the room and personally having a good laugh at this, as was Tommy. The interviewer asked Tommy what his legacy would be and Tommy did not have a clue what he was on about so asked Manny to explain. The 15 minute interview turned into an hour which Tommy wasn't happy about but he was eventually alright with it and went back to his room to rest. I asked the TV guy to forward me the unedited tape of the interview which he did as promised several weeks later.

Tommy was spot on time for the dinner which started with some photos taken by my friend Alan Shaw in the VIP lounge where Ricky Hatton, Alan Minter and Ritchie Woodhall were waiting to meet Tommy and Manny. Mark Peters compèred the show and was very good, but once again they had an auction that went on forever.

My seat was right at the back of the room on a table with a friend from the area, Eric Ragonesi, who had featured Roberto Duran at his club. Eric ran a club and his brother ran a jewellery shop in Birmingham; both were a right laugh and I enjoyed their company. Ken Purchase did his usual thing in going around the tables with the microphone introducing everybody and having a bit of banter with them. I did think he would have given me a mention as he passed by our table although I was not too bothered, but it would have been nice to be acknowledged for bringing two legends in boxing to Telford.

Tommy stood and posed for photos for about an hour then once printed they were coming over and asking Tommy to sign them. He did this for a while but then got fed up with it, so Ricky Hatton's agent Paul Speak moved in and said for Tommy to charge £10 for signings; Tommy appeared to be fine with this now. Paul gave the money to me and I passed it onto Manny, and give him his due, he did offer me something the next morning but I said that was between him and Tommy and took nothing myself.

The next show was at Peterborough with Kevin Sanders.

Kevin's driver Craig turned up at 10 the next morning in a nice Mercedes but I said to him it was going to be a tight squeeze to get our entire luggage in along with me, Tommy and Manny.

Craig somehow managed to get everything in but I had to sit with my case on my knee for the two hour drive to Peterborough. Craig was good crack and Tommy was also very talkative and seemed more relaxed. Manny spoke to me for about an hour on how he had been a time served electrician who then went into sales but boxing was his passion and he could make more money from it. Manny Steward was a really nice guy.

We stopped at a service station for Manny to make a call. As we waited in the car for him he seemed take forever and when he came back Tommy asked him what the hell he had been doing, but Manny joked with him saying it was none of his business and we all had a laugh at him.

On arrival at Peterborough we met Kevin Sanders and he made us all welcome, got our rooms sorted and then asked Tommy to sign a few pairs of gloves. They drove us to the show venue which a huge building. Mark Peters MC'd the show; I sat alongside an ex pro by the name of Lenny Gloster who was nice but very quiet and reserved. Although the meal took a long time Mark Peters kept things flowing well with clips of Tommy's bouts on the big screen. Tommy handled the questions well and Manny was his usual self and could talk forever on boxing.

At most of the shows Manny gave a speech about Tommy saying that he was a just a tall, skinny kid when he first came into the Kronk gym as a 14 year old and never really looked anything special but was very prompt, disciplined and dedicated and then eventually started to win Amateur titles and in 1976 he sparred and many observers said he had the better of Ray Leonard when Ray came to the Kronk whilst he was preparing for the Montreal Olympics. Tommy eventually turned professional and was well supported by all of the Kronk team and Ray Leonard. Manny could not believe that a few years later the two would be involved in one of the biggest fights in boxing history. Manny joked that he and Ray Leonard had a good drink one night and at about 3am in the morning he got Ray to sign a contract to fight Tommy. Losing the fight to Ray Leonard was the biggest disappointment in Manny's life even more than losing his parents, and then after the second fight was given as a draw it was also a massive disappointment especially after Tommy had waited so long to fight Ray and had knocked him down twice but still failed to get the verdict. Tommy knew he had done enough to win the fight but did not complain, and even Ray admitted some years later that Tommy should have been given the verdict. When Tommy fought Hagler he broke his hand in the first round but did not even mention it at the post fight press conference as he did not want to take anything away from Marvin. Tommy tried for a rematch but could not get one. Tommy never lost his power all the way through the weight divisions and he would sell out Las Vegas at all of his fights as fans knew it was going to be exciting whenever Tommy Hearns fought there. Out of all the fighters Manny had worked with over the years Tommy Hearns remained his favourite fighter.

Whilst on the tour Tommy never touched alcohol, just still water and cranberry juice, did not smoke and was very careful with what he ate - used to open sandwiches to see what was in them. He still talked about wanting to win an eighth title. Tommy told me he liked fishing and had a boat on Lake Erie; he had still had two boys at home and lived 15 minutes outside of Detroit with his wife Renee. Muhammad Ali was his favourite fighter, and the hardest hitter he had fought was Hagler, but the toughest was Juan Roldan. Tommy moved down weights to suit Dennis Andries when he became part of the Kronk team and won the Light Heavyweight title. Andries had a massive heart and strength but lacked the skill to keep him at the top.

Kevin Sanders took us to a pub after the show but we just stayed for half an hour as Tommy was tired and would not drink any alcohol and did not like to be in smoky atmospheres.

Tommy knocked for me the next morning to go to breakfast with him and he was very thankful to me for my hospitality and looking after him and said he would like me to promote his next fight over here.

After breakfast we sat in reception awaiting our transport to the next show at Bristol. An elderly guy turned up in reception and came over to me and Tommy and rattled Tommy's career record off as he shook our hands. He said he had come to take us to Bristol. The driver had come in a nice seven seat people carrier. I sat in the back seat, Manny in front of me and then Tommy sat alongside the driver in the front.

As we left the hotel the driver got lost on the first roundabout and then started asking Tommy to navigate for him. Obviously Tommy didn't have a clue so I swapped seats with Tommy to put the guy onto the right road. The driver then took another wrong turning so I suggested that I would drive for him.

So we swapped seats and away we went. Bristol was about a three hour drive so halfway there we stopped at a service station. At the station the elderly driver asked if he could take a photo of us all, and said these were the real photos and said he would send one onto to me later, which he did. Manny said to me that I had made a smart move offering to drive us to Bristol otherwise we may have never got there and thanked me.

We arrived at Bristol at 5.30pm and met up with Chris Sanigar and his son Jamie. Chris got our rooms sorted and then asked me if I could get Tommy and Manny down to the show reception area for 7pm to sign gloves etc. He then gave me a pile of photos and pictures to give to Tommy to sign in his room. Tommy asked me if I could book his flight back to Detroit for him on Sunday as he was not going to Germany with Manny who had Vivian Harris boxing over there. I got on to Jamie from KLM and he then rang me back later to say that he had booked Tommy onto the 1.45 flight from Gatwick to Detroit on Sunday. This meant that I would have to take Tommy there and then get back to Newcastle.

Tommy and Manny came down to the reception and Tommy signed all kinds of gloves and photos for Chris; he said they were going to start the dinner and wanted us to come back down at 9.30. Jamie gave me a bag of pictures for Tommy to sign in his room. Tommy did not appear too happy with this but took them anyway.

We came down to the function room on time and the question and answer session went quite well with Tommy and Manny as good as ever. The photo session was done by Les Clark this time, who also worked at Dave Furnish's shows. As soon as the photos were finished Tommy and Manny retired to their rooms, and I went back down for a drink with one of Chris Sanigar's trainers Nigel Christian, and Les Clark and had a good laugh with them at their tales from the fight scene.

We took a cab to Bristol train station and I went and bought our tickets to London where Lee Short and Charlie Magri were doing the next and final show. The carriage was excellent with loads of room, and we all took a double seat each. Tommy was starting to relax now as he knew this was the last show and he would soon be on his way home to Detroit.

Lee and Charlie picked us up in a massive black limousine, which struggled to get through the London traffic, but Lee and Charlie made us laugh as they gave commentary on a guided tour of some of the sights on our way to the Britannia Hotel.

The hotel was absolutely fabulous and my room overlooked the river with fantastic views. The bathroom had a Jacuzzi in it and the TV set was huge. Tommy's room was the presidential suite which was massive and actually had a metal spiral staircase going up to his room. Tommy asked me if he could have it changed to another room but I persuaded him to stay there as it was only for one night. Charlie gave me a box of programmes for Tommy and Manny to sign so I gave half to Tommy and half to Manny. I went into the room with Tommy and he laughed when he saw all of the programmes, but I said it was the last show and for him to do his best. Tommy started signing and I noticed he just signed Tommy Hearns now and left out the 'Hit Man' piece and small motif that he was used to doing on the gloves and pictures. Tommy was good company now and I felt a lot more relaxed with him; we became friends. There was a knock on his door and it was the porter with a letter for Tommy. Tommy asked me to open it and it was a couple of postcards from fans wanting his autograph. Tommy politely signed them both and said he did not mind.

We went down into the VIP area and met up with Charlie Magri and Lee Short. Alan Minter and his son Ross were there and also John 'The Beast' Mugabi who had a war with Marvin Hagler. John called Tommy over and asked if he would fight him and started sparring up with him for a laugh.

In the function room I sat on the top table alongside Tommy and it was a nice relaxed atmosphere. Michael Watson was there with his carer and I told Tommy what had happened to Michael in his bout with Chris Eubank. When Michael was introduced to the audience Tommy got down from the top table and went over to shake Michael's hand; this was a lovely gesture from Tommy that went down well with the audience. Brian Doogan, a sports writer, who rang me from time to time to ask about boxing legends I had dealt with, had called and asked me if he could do a quick interview with Tommy, so as it was the last night I invited him to the show. Brian was a charming Irish guy but was insistent on getting what he wanted. He came to the top table and interviewed Tommy whilst the others were having their meal. Brian put his Dictaphone recorder on the table in front of Tommy, but after a while Tommy picked it up and said to him you will have enough now, man, letting Brian know that he had had enough.

The evening auction started and halfway through it Tommy took the microphone and started talking real fast like a proper auctioneer and then after calling out numbers he shouted SOLD! and had the audience in stitches of laughter.

The following morning I rang Tommy at 9.00am but he mumbled that he was still in bed and asked me to wait for him in the breakfast area. I then got a call from Manny saying that he was already at the breakfast area. I had a chat with Manny and he was extremely gracious and thankful to me for organising the tour and after we had said our farewells he then took a taxi to Heathrow for his flight to Germany. I had to get Tommy to Gatwick so I asked Lee if he knew anyone who might give us a lift. Lee had a couple of friends who had attended the event that were driving that way so they very kindly said they would take us to Gatwick. I was sitting with Tommy having breakfast when I got a call from my brother

Bryan saying that not to worry but our mother had taken ill on her trip to Blackpool and was in hospital – but it did obviously worry me and now I could not wait to get home.

Lee's pal and his wife drove Tommy and me to Gatwick and Tommy started talking more than ever in the car and was hilarious when he started joking with the driver's wife.

At Gatwick Tommy hugged me and said he wanted to give me his home phone number which he did as he wanted me to keep in touch with him and he got quite emotional as this was the first trip of this kind that he had ever done in the UK. Tommy went for his flight to Detroit and I then took the shuttle over to Heathrow.

As I left Tommy I got a lump in my throat, a similar feeling to leaving Roberto Duran – maybe the satisfaction of completing the tour but also realising that Tommy Hearns, a world boxing legend who had shared the ring with the likes of Leonard, Duran, Hagler and Benitez, had become a friend to just a joiner from Jarrow. I still give Tommy a call from time to time and went out to see him in Detroit during 2007.

THOMAS HEARNS, MARTYN AND MANNY STEWARD, 2004

THOMAS HEARNS AND MARTYN, 2004

TOMMY AND MANNY WITH PROMOTER LEE MALONEY AT LIVERPOOL, 2004

*THOMAS HEARNS, MARTYN, MANNY STEWARD & DRIVER
AT MOTORWAY CAFÉ ON WAY TO BRISTOL, 2004*

*THOMAS HEARNS, MANNY STEWARD, DAMIAN MCCANN & 2015 WORLD
MIDDLEWEIGHT CHAMPION ANDY LEE OPENING BELFAST KRONK GYM, 2004*

ON TOUR WITH SUGAR RAY LEONARD

After touring with Roberto Duran I thought I would push the boat out and try to get the legendary former six time world champion Sugar Ray Leonard to come over and tour the country. Sugar Ray was always a big favourite of mine but a close friend of mine said he imagined Leonard would cost a fortune, be too demanding and be out of my league.

Sugar Ray Leonard was born Ray Charles Leonard on 17 May 1956 in Rocky Mount, North Carolina.

He was the flamboyant technical boxer who took over the void left in boxing by Muhammad Ali and ignited the public interest in boxing. Ray had a brilliant amateur career, and went on to win the light welterweight gold medal in the 1976 Olympics in Montreal where he charmed the crowds with his blistering hand speed combination punching, along with his tasselled boots that carried a photo of his girlfriend attached. After turning professional aged 20, Ray won 25 fights before winning his first world title at Welterweight by defeating the brilliant defensive technician Wilfred Benitez in a cat and mouse 15-round contest. In Ray's first defence he KO'd Dave Boy Green in round four, but then suffered his first career defeat against the Panamanian former lightweight king Roberto 'Hands of Stone' Duran in a bout titled the 'Brawl in Montreal' for his WBC welterweight crown. Ray avenged this defeat just five months later in the famous 'No Mas' fight in New Orleans. On 16th June 1981 Ray challenged Tommy Hearns for a fight billed the 'Showdown' which was for Tommy's WBA welterweight title and Ray's WBC version of the crown. After 12 rounds of classic technical boxing, Ray was behind on points and his left eye was closing rapidly as he struggled to overcome Tommy's rapier like left jab but amazingly after being told by his corner man Angelo Dundee that he "was blowing it" Ray went out blasting in the thirteenth round and his punches had Tommy staggering around the ring. Ray did the same in the next round and the referee finally stepped in to stop the contest to save Tommy from further punishment. After this fight Ray developed a detached retina and retired from the sport. After three years out during which time middleweight king Marvelous Marvin Hagler was the one to beat, Ray decided to come back and challenge Marvin in one of the biggest fights in boxing history. Sugar Ray amazingly outsmarted and outboxed Marvin to gain a split decision over 12 rounds to claim the prestigious middleweight title. During the contest Ray's lightning combinations caught the judge's eyes and gave him the nod over the advancing Hagler. The result of this bout will always be controversial, but as Ray will tell you boxing is about hitting your opponent and not getting hit back and that is what Leonard did for most of the bout, although Marvin forced the fight from the first bell until the last. Ray went on to win titles at Super-middleweight and Light Heavyweight before retiring in 1997 with a record of 40 fights, 36 wins, just three losses and one draw, with 25 KOs.

THE CONTACT

I checked out Ray Leonard's agent by way of my international boxing contacts and was put in touch with his man at the time, Bjorn Rebney. Bjorn was very professional with his correspondence and we negotiated contract terms over several months, but the fee they were looking at appeared to be way out of my reach. After sitting on it for some time I played with figures and tested the water with other promoters. By way of interest I then decided to give it a go and negotiated with Bjorn one more time. To feature him in Newcastle I would have to charge £100 per ticket, so I reckoned the only way to do this was to break it up and get a £50 deposit first and then the balance closer to the time. After a series of adverts I had a fairly good response and decided to give it a go.

Bjorn Rebney then sent over a four page contract which was one sided, but after negotiating the bullet points, it became workable and as I was used to contracts now I did add in a few things that I thought he would object to but he agreed to it all. The biggest difference with Ray Leonard was that a large deposit had to be made before he left America and the balance paid into a trust account which was payable on his arrival here. I had to work very hard to persuade other promoters to accept this, and a few pulled out as these terms were unacceptable to them.

I eventually had six shows set up at Newcastle, Bradford, Sheffield, Telford, Manchester, Bristol and London with deposits paid by five – all but Manchester. The guy there appeared fine but when it came to getting the deposit he became hard to contact. So I informed Bjorn of this but he insisted that he would need that show to have the agreed fee in place.

So the only way around this was to stage the show myself at Manchester. I did have a few contacts there but not a lot. I decided to start advertising as a feeler and then made a visit to a venue there. I used the Michael Brodie fight at the MEN arena to kill two birds with one stone, and visited Old Trafford as the chosen venue. The venue was fine but nothing special and the staff there were not very supportive at all and just talked money and numbers. I also advertised in the show programmes for the Brodie and Matthew Hatton fights around that time, but did not have a great response.

I drove down to watch the Brodie fight but it was a poor fight, not very well attended and I drove home and watched the last few rounds on TV.

Everything was now in place; all that was due was to finalise contracts and make the first deposit.

For some strange reason during February 2004 Bjorn Rebney became hard to contact and although he had given me his personal mobile number and home number, as much as I tried I could not make contact with him, and the Sugar Ray Leonard office became just an answer machine reply. Weeks went by and then I spotted a news flash on the fight news website. It stated that Bjorn Rebney was suing Sylvester Stallone and Mark Burnett who were the producers of a new boxing reality show called The Contender which also had Sugar Ray Leonard as a mentor with Stallone. It stated that Rebney was claiming damages because they had enticed Leonard away from him, causing SRL Boxing cooperation to close down. So I now gathered why I could not contact him.

The Contender was a new boxing programme in the US that featured struggling boxers and gave them the chance of prize money and recognition.

I contacted Ray Leonard's personal secretary, a Miss Caren Kinder. Caren appeared to be charming and confirmed that Ray and Bjorn had parted ways and that she would put me in touch with Ray's new lawyer Mr Elliott Kleinberg.

At least now I had the confirmation in writing that Ray Leonard was not going ahead with the tour. I checked this out with Caren Kinder and she did then confirm that Ray had split with Rebney and that there was no way he could now commit himself to the tour. So now I had to immediately inform all the interested promoters and those purchasing tickets of the cancellation. This was a complete nightmare and made you feel very unprofessional, but the situation was totally out of my hands.

In times like that you have to pick up the pieces and move on, as much as you feel like chucking it all in and saying never again.

It was at this time that I thought about turning to Manny Steward who had previously enquired about coming over with Tommy Hearns to fill the dates booked for Sugar Ray. I contacted Manny and he was fine with it.

After the Hearns tour I had already done the hard work with contracts etc and was put in touch with Ray's new lawyer Elliott Kleinberg. Elliot came across as a God-like type of lawyer, and I had to make a special appointment to speak to him by way of a conference call; however when this did happen he came across as a nice type of guy and said that he and Ray apologised for the circumstances and that Ray would hopefully do the tour the following year, if he could be released from the Contender programme for a week.

Although it had taken a few years to put together, everything was now set for Ray to come over for one week during October 2005. This was the big one. Sugar Ray Leonard had been involved in some of the greatest ever fights with Duran, Hagler Hearns, Benitez and many more and just always had that extra touch of class and professionalism about him. Although the first show date was booked for a Saturday night at Newcastle, Elliott informed me that Ray would want to come in two days early so that it would help him adjust to our time differences. I knew this was an extra cost for hotel bills etc but this was Sugar Ray Leonard and this was big.

When all travel was booked, Ray was set to travel with his son Ray Jr and was due in to Newcastle on the Thursday at around 4.30pm.

Waiting at Newcastle Airport was again a massive worry but oddly enough I was not as worried this time as awaiting Duran or Tommy Hearns even though I felt Sugar Ray was the bigger name. I was then informed by staff that there were problems with the KLM flight from LA via Amsterdam and he was delayed for two hours due to an air conditioning problem – the flight had apparently taken off and then had to return to the airport and was now scheduled to land at 18.00hrs. At the airport there is not much to do apart from reading a few magazines and drinking coffee which costs a small fortune along with the parking, so it looked like I had to do this for another couple of hours.

It came up on the board that the plane had now landed and it suddenly hit me as to how the hell had I pulled this one off, bringing one of the all time greatest names in boxing to Newcastle. As the arrivals started coming through the gates I spotted Ray immediately, wearing a baseball cap, smart black casual jacket and jogging bottoms. I could not believe how small he looked, but it was definitely him, the guy who had won the hearts of Americans by winning the Olympic Gold medal whilst wearing a photo of his girlfriend Juanita Wilkinson on his white tasselled boots and then going on to become a five weight world champion sharing the ring with Benitez, Duran, Hearns and Hagler and beating them all. Ray had obviously seen a photo of me, probably on the fighting talk website, and came over and hugged me straight away. His son Ray Jr accompanied him and was a lot bigger than I expected and we all shook hands and they then followed me to the awaiting luxury people carrier with the blacked out windows that I had hired for our transportation. A wave of relief came over me but also the worry of what Ray would really be like and how I would handle this for a week travelling across the country.

A funny thing happened as we drove through the town on the way to the Copthorne Hotel on Newcastle's Quayside. I was sitting in the front of the people carrier alongside the driver and Ray sat directly behind me with Ray Jr next to him. We chatted for a while about Ray's flight problems and then Ray asked me how long it had been since I first made contact with him about the tour. I then turned around directly facing him and said it must have been nearly two years since I had first contacted Bjorn Rebney and then there was the issue with the Contender. Ray immediately raised his voice and said, "Hey Martyn, please keep your eyes on the road." I laughed out loud at this as it was only then that he realised we drove on the other side over here as he obviously thought I was driving when I had turned around to talk to him. We all had a real good laugh about this and it put us all in a relaxed mood. I chatted with Ray about a few things on the boxing scene and he came across as a really nice guy. I think as Ray was also the same age as me it also helped us get along and feel comfortable with each other. We checked into the hotel and Ray said could we meet for dinner at about 7.30pm which was fine by me.

Ray was spot on time and there were actually just the three of us in the restaurant at the Copthorne Hotel. Ray joked with the young waitress and asked if it was always this busy. Ray asked about previous tours with Duran and Hearns that I had done and he and Ray Jr laughed at some of the stories I told him. He asked about what I did for a living, the gym I run and about my family. Ray and Ray Jr also told me some good stories about his big fights and we all had a good laugh and all appeared to get along with each other. I asked Ray if he wanted to go for a stroll along Newcastle quayside and Ray was fine with this. We walked and then as it was a little chilly we popped into a bar called the Blue Velvet club where there happened to be music and dancing girls on, then from there we headed back to the hotel but decided to call into Sea Nightclub which was on the way back, on Newcastle's quayside. As it was a Thursday night the club was quiet and I was pleased no one recognised Ray. We chatted at the bar counter and then after a few drinks Ray Jr decided to have a dance. At that point one of the door staff recognised me through my boxing connections and asked if that was Ray Leonard I was with. Initially I was going to say no, but then another doorman came over and asked Ray to sign for him so I had to say yes it was Ray Leonard. After a few minutes word travelled and they were all coming over and asking to have their photos taken and then somehow one of the photos with the door staff appeared up on a big screen in the club. At first I was worried Ray would be bothered by it all but as it did not appear to, I felt ok about it. We strolled back to our hotel at about 1.30am and turned in. I woke as usual at about 6.30am and showered and went for breakfast at about 7.30.

The plan for the day was to maybe show Ray around Newcastle but I wanted to get him to call into the gym and meet the young boxers and then hopefully meet Linda and Joy and then go for a meal with friends Paddy Murray and John Devlin whose pal ran the Mill House Pub where we would be looked after.

I thought Ray would be up at about 10am but he and Ray Jr were asleep until well after midday. One of the maids knocked and asked me if I could get his autograph for her, so I asked her to look into his room for me which she did and said both of them were still in bed. I knew they would have jet lag but wondered how the hell they could sleep for this long? Maybe they had taken a few sleeping tablets to help them get over the jet lag and prepare them for the tour. I asked my friend Paddy Murray to borrow a decent set of wheels and he turned up in his sister's X5 to take us to do our gym visit. Paddy turned up at about 5pm which was ok as the gym session did not usually start until 6.30pm. I gave Ray a call and he said he would be down at about 5.30pm. On the way to the gym Ray asked where I lived so I told him it was only five minutes from the gym so thought it a good opportunity to take him home and meet Linda and Joy which he was fine with. When I knocked on the door Linda answered and her face lit up when she saw Ray and Ray Jr, I then introduced them to Joy, my 13 year old daughter, who didn't really have a clue who Ray was or how much of a world boxing legend he was. We went through into our bar area and Ray took a look at all of the photos of the champions I had featured but some of them he did not know. Ray, Ray Jr and Paddy had a few soft drinks and then posed for a few photos before leaving for the gym.

At the gym I had informed a few of the boxers that I might be getting Sugar Ray to come over but could not guarantee it as I did not know what Ray would be like, but as it was a training night they would be there anyway and my fellow coach Paul Harkness who was excellent would be taking the session. I also invited Mick Worrall, sports editor for the local South Shields Gazette newspaper, to come with a photographer. Mick was a very good journalist and had been sports editor at the Gazette for several years and could put an excellent boxing piece together, and I always invited him to my boxing dinner shows after which he would always give a good write up.

At the gym Ray watched the youngsters spar a round each and then gave them advice and posed for photos with them and signed autographs – and was absolutely excellent. Although some of the young boxers were too young to really appreciate the legendary status of Ray, most were overwhelmed by his presence. Ray Jr recorded some of them on his phone video and then showed them it, and they are felt great watching it.

Paddy drove us straight from the gym to the Mill House pub near Gateshead where we met up with John Devlin and his pal Alan 'Dobba' Dobson who was going to take over the driving.

The meal was fine and John had previously met Ray on the QE2 some years ago when he was working on it as a joiner and Ray was travelling on board whilst making a documentary for a US TV network. They told the story about when they set up a makeshift boxing ring and the ship's cook got in the ring with Ray and Ray dropped him with a body shot after the cook got a bit heavy handed.

After our meal Dobba drove us over to Sea nightclub where we had been the previous night and this time we were given a private area upstairs. It was busier this time but after word got round that Ray was in we got a bit pestered and Ray asked to go back to the hotel.

On the Saturday I had arranged for us to be picked up at 1.30pm by Dobba to go to the Sunderland v Manchester United game. I thought with it being such a big game in the area it would be good to get Ray introduced on the pitch in front of 48,000 fans. I dealt with a girl by the name of Louise at Sunderland and she was excellent from the moment we arrived. Louise met us on arrival and took us straight down to where the Sunderland players where getting prepared in the changing area. She then took us to a small room where both team managers, Sir Alex Ferguson for Manchester United and Mick McCarthy for Sunderland, were standing having a chat and watching a live game on TV. Ray was very courteous with them both and posed for photos but did not have a clue who either of them were. Sir Alex mentioned something to me and Ray about the Hagler fight but Ray just laughed it off and probably could not understand Sir Alex's broad Scottish accent.

Louise then took us into the Sunderland players' dressing room where they were getting rubbed down with liniment and warming themselves up, but even I did not have a clue who any of them were so there was no way Ray would; nevertheless a few of them came over and shook our hands. Louise then asked if Ray would go out onto the pitch before the team came out and asked if he would wear a Sunderland shirt over the top of his own tee shirt to which he kindly obliged. Ray went out onto the pitch and I followed. He got a great reception from the crowd and it was an amazing experience for me to hear it from 48,000 fans. Ray signed a few autographs for the kids at the front and then we stood and watched as the two teams walked out past us. I was amazed at how tall Christiano Ronaldo was.

Louise then took us back up into the box stand where food and drink was provided for us. The game was just actually starting to warm up after about 15 minutes when Ray said he to me he had seen enough and asked to be taken back to the hotel. As it happened I heard later that Manchester United won 2-0.

We drove back to the hotel and Ray signed the gloves and picture items for the show auction and photos. I left Ray and Ray Jr at the hotel and told them that I would pick them back up at about 8.30. This was timed so that the dinner at the show would be over and so that Ray was not sitting awaiting everyone to finish eating. Ray was ready on time and I took him through the back entrance of the hotel away from autograph hunters at the main hotel entrance.

Although the fanfare was messed up by the young hotel staff, Steve Holdsworth MC'd the show and gave Ray a great entrance into the room where he received a tremendous reception from the diners. Ray thanked me for having him over and thanked all of the fans for turning out to see him, and then Steve Holdsworth took questions from the fans to Ray. Ray answered the questions professionally and did not duck any. The photo session was slow to start but once Linda came in she organised it brilliantly and got things moving on a one-in-one-out basis. Linda was very good at this and would be nice to people as much as possible but when they were full of drink and becoming a nuisance she would move them on very quickly and did not take any nonsense from anybody. Linda was teetotal and could be as sharp as a tack with her wit, so this always helped.

The memorabilia dealers were out in force again but our door staff were told not to let anyone into the photo room with gloves to be signed as they usually ended up for sale on eBay the next day.

After the show we went back to the hotel and went into the bar for a drink. There happened to be a wedding taking place and obviously word went quickly around the Ray Leonard was in the bar. A guy came over and chatted with us and told us that they also called him Ray Leonard. We all had a good laugh about this, but I did quietly ask a few of his company about this and they all confirmed he was called Ray Leonard. As it was now well past midnight we turned into bed as we were being picked up at noon the following day for the drive to Sheffield to Glyn Rhodes's show. It was a comfortable drive in a Mercedes Viano I had hired and as we left Ray asked if we could pop into the McDonald's drive through in the Westerhope area as we left Newcastle This assured me that Ray was ok and did not demand the best, in way of restaurants etc.

At Sheffield we met Glyn and his beautiful wife Hilary with their two gorgeous kids Jorgen and Joseph. Glyn took his ten items to Ray's room to be signed but found out that they had taped the backs on the frames so me and him were struggling like hell to get the backs off to enable Ray to sign them. Glyn came at 8.30pm to pick us up in a black jeep to take us to the show which was held at Sheffield Wednesday football club. The dinner was still on so we hung around for about an hour in a VIP area were Ray spoke with a few young boxers and signed their items for them. In the function room they had a boxing ring set up and Ray spoke and answered questions from the ring where a couple of the young lads had been doing an exhibition earlier. Ray did well and then we went into a room where the photos and autographs took place. Glyn had the security very tight and then took us back to the hotel where we sat and had a chat.

Ray said he did not want to leave until 2pm the following day for the trip to Manchester where we would meet up with Wally Dixon, the show promoter. I rang Wally and informed him of this and he said his transport would be there for us. Wally arrived with Paul Speak who was Ricky Hatton's agent and they were in two large jeeps. We were driven to the Renaissance Hotel and Paul gave Ray a massive box containing about 400 photos for him to sign in his room.

They told us to be ready to be picked up for 6.30pm for the dinner function that was to be held at Old Trafford cricket club. A large people carrier turned up to take us to the function room; Wally had to sit on my knee as there was no room for him. At the club Wally had a VIP area set up where fans could have a photo taken with Ray before the dinner; this seemed to take forever.

The show's master of ceremonies was boxer's artist Brian Meadows who introduced us all as we entered the room and did give me a good mention. There were probably about 400 diners in the room but very little security. As we were sat at the top table diners kept coming up with gloves to be signed and Ray was getting annoyed about this, but just tried to keep everybody happy. They sat Ray next to Ricky Hatton. Ricky gave his usual speech and as I had noticed Ray was getting cheesed off with fans asking for signings, I had a word with Wally and Paul Speak but it made very little difference. I got a tap on the shoulder and Ray Fisher, a promoter from that area whom I had been dealing with but never met introduced himself to me and said to me that "I told you that it would end up like this". As more and more fans came up, the top table nearly fell over so Ray decided he had had enough and asked to leave. We exited out of the rear door and went back to the hotel. We ordered a few pizzas and sat and chatted with a few guys who happened to be staying at the hotel and had a good laugh.

All Star Signings turned up as agreed at about 11.30am with bags full of gloves to be signed. They said 300 gloves and I was amazed at how many bags it took to hold all of the gloves. Although Ray had a late night we set the signing up in his room and he speedily got through them all with no problems and was very professional.

Wally kept ringing me to ask if Ray would go to Arnie's gym and then go to watch Ricky training. I put this to Ray but he said that he felt we only had time to go to Ricky's gym as he was tired and it had been very late when we all got to bed. Paul Speak picked us up at 2.45 and we drove to Ricky's gym. The gym was a bit of a dump with just about six bags, a ring and a beam that Ricky used for jumping over. Ricky had finished training but Ray took time to chat to him and Billy Graham his trainer. On the way back to the hotel they made a detour and visited Arnie (Anthony Farnell's gym); this gym was excellent with all new equipment and a new ring. Ray posed for photos at both gyms.

As we had a free night, we were taken for a meal to Phil's restaurant (Lounge 10) which was apparently where all the stars dined when in Manchester. I sat with Paul Speak and we were entertained by a jazz singer and also a table magician. A promoter and trainer Jack Trickett and his much younger wife sat with us. Jack was good crack and told some good tales. We left and went back to the renaissance hotel and sat till about 1.30 having a chat.

The following morning the next show promoter Ken Purchase turned up at about 11.45, along with Joe Egan and a couple of heavies. Ken came in a minibus and also a van to carry our luggage. Ray and Ray Jr came down at about 12.30 for our journey to Birmingham. Big Joe Egan kept us all amused during the journey with his Irish banter and told some great tales. He rang Nigel Benn from his mobile and Frank Bruno and passed the phone to Ray to say hello to them both. We stopped off at a body builder's gym and posed for a few photos with Joe and his pals. Ken got Ray to sign a few items in the van and then Paul Speak asked me to get Ray down to the press room for 7pm. The boxing journalist Brian

Doogan appeared and asked if he could do a quick interview with Ray in his room, and then gate crashed the show. Brian was a nice guy but was in Ray's face too much and Ray was getting a little uneasy with him. In the function room Ken once again sat me at the back of the room with my old pal Eric Ragonesi and his brother. Mark Peters MC'd the show and introduced John H Stracey who sang both the American and our own national anthems and was very good. Kevin Lueshing and Steve Collins were also on the top table. The Spearmint Rhino girls were out in force doing the raffle sales. Ray spoke well and gave me a thank you for bringing him over. The photo session was run by darts player Phil Taylor and somehow ended up a shambles. We went to Spearmint Rhino with Mark Peters and Kevin Lueshing but it was poor and I only stayed for an hour and then went back to the hotel at 1am.

I had breakfast with Brian Doogan and then Ray's former opponent Dave 'Boy' Green turned up to take Ray and Ray Jr over to his house near Peterborough where the next show was due. I travelled over myself with Ray's luggage in a people carrier. I then met up with John H Stracey in the foyer and he told me that he had had an argument with Dave Boy Green the previous night over the use of his head when they boxed each other years ago.

At Peterborough I met up with the promoter Kevin Sanders and his lovely wife Vivienne – they were a nice couple. A guy from Soccer AM, Graham Lewis, was making repeated calls to me for to do a five minute spot with Ray at the hotel. Ray agreed to do it but Kevin was not too happy about it, as these guys always take a lot longer than they say. London promoter Lee Short then gave me a call to ask if I could try and give his show a lift as he was struggling with ticket sales. The TV guy was calling me constantly and said they had booked a room at the Marriott where we were staying and the interview would only take five minutes. I smoothed this over with Kevin Sanders.

As it happened I made sure I sat in on the interview and it was only about five minutes and Ray was excellent with them. I met up with two former British champion boxers Billy Schwer and Mickey Cantwell in the foyer. We had a short chat and they were both smashing guys.

The show went ok and I sat next to the area's top amateur boxer Michael McGuire who has since turned professional. Colin Hart gave Ray a great welcome and said out of all of the champions over the past 30 years or so, Ray Leonard was the best. Mark Peters did his usual stuff and his PA system was excellent. The photo session went ok but once again took too long and then after they were printed Ray was asked to sign them, but he was fine with this.

We then went back to the Marriott hotel and I sat with Colin Hart and Dave Green while Ray and Ray Jr went back to their rooms to get changed out of their suits.

Ray and Ray Jr came down after about 15 minutes and joined us for a chat which was excellent. Ray was totally down to earth. Ray and Ray Jr asked to use the toilets and both disappeared for about 15 minutes. Colin asked me to go and check on them as they had been away too long. When I went into the toilets Ray and Ray Jr were sitting on the wash basin tables chatting and I asked if all was ok. They said fine and came out with me. Ray then asked me where we were going the following day and how long it would take. He then started talking aggressively and this was very noticeable to Colin and Dave Green and myself. Colin then said to me that he wondered if something had happened whilst in the toilets as Ray was not normally like that. Ray and Ray Jr then retired to their rooms and I sat with Colin for about an hour and he told some great boxing stories and is a great guy.

The following morning Glenn Catley and his pal turned up in a nice People Carrier to take us to Bristol for Chris Sanigar's show. The back seats were facing each other and I knew I struggled to sit like that so asked if I could squeeze into the front with Glenn and his pal. Glenn was a former world middleweight champion whom I had the pleasure of meeting on the Duran tour and a nice guy. He was now running a removal business and his phone never stopped ringing. The journey took about three hours but Ray was ok and got some rest. When we arrived at Bristol we met up with promoter Chris Sanigar and his son Jamie. Ray asked if they could get him a book on the history of Bristol for his daughter. Ray did try to get one at each city we arrived in.

I took a walk into the city and got myself a snack and then after having a look around decided to head back but got lost. I asked a lady to direct me to the Marriott only to be informed that there were two Marriott hotels in Bristol and I was at the wrong one, so had to walk for a while to get to the other one.

Chris had set it up for Ray to come into the room after the meal which worked well and he went straight into the question and answer session hosted by Steve Holdsworth. The session here was the longest out of all of the shows. The photo session was well organised and Chris, as organised as ever, moved anybody on quickly who was taking too long. Ray and I went upstairs to a bar area after the show and sat chatting with a few young lads who really knew their boxing. Chris Sanigar also joined us later and was very nice and appreciative of my efforts at getting Ray to come over.

We went to Bristol station and took the train to London. I booked first class seating which was excellent and Ray slept most of the way. I received a call from a reporter to say that he was putting a piece in a Sunday newspaper and would mention about the fee Ray was getting. I said that would not be a good idea and informed him that it was bad manners to do that and that if he did we would make sure he would not get access to Ray again. I asked him to ring me back to confirm that he would take it out, which he did.

We met up with Lee Short and Charlie Magri at Euston Station and they took us to a huge black limousine. On the way to the hotel we had set it up for us to stop off at the famous Repton boys club in London. I met up with the club leader Tony Burns whom I had previously met during my own boxing days as I had boxed a couple of his Repton boxers in my own career.

Tony asked me to say hello to Frankie Deans who was my first boxing coach and a good friend of Tony's in the north east. Ray watched the lads training and took a skipping rope and did an amazing routine for them. He also signed the gym wall for them, and I wished that I had asked him to do this at our gym. We then went over to the Peacock gym which was a lot quieter as there were only a couple of lads in training at the time.

We then drove to the Britannia Hotel and checked in; there was some kind of mix up with the rooms but Lee Short eventually got it sorted out. I received a call from Ronald McIntosh to ask if he could do a 10 minute interview with Ray for BBC TV. Ray was ok with this so long as it was only 10 minutes. I set this up with Ray and we both went together into the room Ronald had booked. Ray was excellent and Ronald said afterwards that he did not have to do even one retake during filming as Ray was perfect. He did ask if he could do another five minutes on boxing and Ray asked if it was ok with me, which I thought was very kind of him – a superstar in world boxing asking a Jarrow lad if it was ok by me. At the VIP area we met up with Sylvia Spensley and her husband whom Caren Kinder had arranged to meet up with Ray from a previous acquaintance. At the function I sat next to Dave Boy Green. During the meal I said to Lee that it may be a good idea to take Ray over and get the photos done for anyone who wanted them; this appeared to work fine. The question and answer session went well and then they had a Del Boy lookalike guy do the auction but he didn't go down that well. They then had a Tina Turner tribute act on that was very good and Ray had a dance and was very relaxed now that the tour was over. John H Stracey sang a couple of songs and once again was very good. I sat with Lee Short and a few of his pals until about 5am.

Lee took Ray over to Heathrow airport and I took Ray Jr over to Gatwick for their respective flights. Ray Jr wore the Spennymoor top Robbie Ellis had given him so I asked him for a quick photo to send to Robbie that I am sure would please him and the Spennymoor lads. I caught the train home from King's Cross to Newcastle.

Although a great relief when it's all over, this had been the big one with probably boxing's biggest name of his era and I found out that he was as just as down to earth as the others and a real nice guy.

*SUGAR RAY MEETING MISS JOY DEVLIN (12YRS) AT
MARTYN'S HOME IN JARROW, 2005*

SUGAR RAY AND MRS LINDA DEVLIN, 2005

RAY LEONARD JNR, MARTYN AND SUGAR RAY
LEONARD AT NEWCASTLE NIGHTCLUB, 2005

SUGAR RAY ON PIANO AT MILL HOUSE PUB, GATESHEAD, 2005

SUGAR RAY LEONARD AT BILTON HALL GYM, JARROW WITH YOUNG BOXERS

SUGAR RAY AT GYM WITH BILTON HALL BOXERS, JARROW, 2005

RAY LEONARD MEETING RICKY HATTON AT MANCHESTER GYM, 2005

RAY LEONARD MEETING WITH FORMER OPPONENT DAVE BOY GREEN, 2005

PROMOTER KEN PURCHASE, RAY LEONARD, AND PHIL TAYLOR, BIRMINGHAM, 2005

RAY LEONARD AND PROMOTER CHRIS SANIGAR, BRISTOL, 2005

ANOTHER TOUR WITH SUGAR RAY

After months of dealings with various promoters planning another tour for Ray during 2006, I organised for Ray to arrive at Newcastle Airport on Thursday 12th October at midday. Ray arrived alone but said his publicist Emily Snider had to return for her passport and would arrive later. As we drove down to the hotel we chatted about the current state of boxing and how it needed a lift. We agreed to meet at the hotel for dinner at 8pm. We chatted about our families and what we were both up to. Ray said he was still busy with the Contender programme and had not touched any alcohol for about 60 days, as he had to be switched on at all times. We both retired to our rooms about 10pm as Ray was tired after his long journey.

I had breakfast on the Saturday and rang Ray at 11.15 and asked him if he wanted to go for a stroll along the quayside as it was a beautiful day. He said he would go for a workout at the gym and give me a call me later. Lee from All Star Signings turned up at 1.30 for a signing session. I tried calling Ray and went to his room but later found him in the hotel gym lifting a few weights; he was all alone and had his headphones on. Ray said he would shower and then come up to sign Lee's items. We chatted as Ray did the signings and he told us about how he had turned 50 and had a party. He then went to his room and brought a DVD player out with clips of his party, at which a lot of the guests were film stars and in fancy dress. I ran up to Dawson & Sanderson to sort out some dollars and when I came back I met a lovely American blonde in the lift who just happened to be Ray's publicist Emily Snider who had just arrived.

We travelled to the show at the Roker Hotel, Sunderland and I had all of our club boxers there to meet Ray in their white shirts. I also had a couple of pals, Brian and Jason Weightman to help out with the show security. Dave Greener MC'd the show and was his usual self but did forget to mention the top table guests. My pal Dobba drove Ray to the venue to arrive after dinner and was bang on time. Ray took the microphone and thanked all in attendance for coming and myself for organising the tour and then asked the audience to fire any questions at him about his fights and career. Ray handled this well and then we presented him with a birthday cake to mark his 50th. My daughter Joy and her friend Gabrielle did the honours. I also had Ray present our young boxers with new head guards which he had bought for them from an interview fee I had organised on the previous tour. The show went well and Ray was very impressed as I had arranged it so there was no hanging about for him: he came in, went straight into this speech, questions and answers, photos and then away. He said that was the way he would like all of the shows to be but I knew that would not happen.

The following morning we met up at 10.30am for our pick up to Newcastle airport for the flight to London. The flight was only an hour and we were met at the airport by former British Heavyweight champion Scott Welsh who was promoting the next show at Brighton, just an hour's drive from London. Scott arrived in a massive Hummer limousine and he was accompanied by Joe Egan who provided the chat and entertainment. As we travelled down to Brighton we stopped off at a hospital to visit a friend of Scott's who was in there and having treatment for cancer. Ray was very good with this and handled it well. We arrived at the hotel about 5pm and Ray and Emily were very tired with the travel. Scott requested to me to have Ray downstairs for 6.30pm to pose for photos with guests. Alan from KO promotions handled this and he was very professional. We all went into the main hall and there was an amateur boxing show on. I was approached by Mick Degnan and my good friend Chris Robson, coach from Bishop Auckland ABC, who had a boxer on the bill. Lewis Cope was boxing against Ben Murphy from Brighton but lost a points decision. The show was ok but once again the dinner took too long to serve and it was very late before the boxing started. Tyson Fury was also supposed to be on the bill but pulled out for some reason. After the boxing and entertainment and then an auction that brought good money in, Ray got in the boxing ring with Mark Peters and did his interview from there and was very good, his usual self.

The following morning Scott Welsh called me to ask Ray to come to his room to sign the memorabilia for him; we then went down and had breakfast with Scott and his partner and he asked if we would call into Scott's gym. The gym was on Brighton's sea front area and Ray met up with the amateurs and showed them a few moves and did his skipping routine for them which was absolute class, although he struggled due to the low ceiling. As the next show was not until the Monday at Gatwick, Ray had arranged to meet some people in London for a business meeting and was being picked up at midday. He asked me if I wanted to go with them or meet them at Gatwick. I said I would go into London with them to save any mix up as the Gatwick promoter could then pick us all up together.

When the people carrier arrived to pick us up it was a driver for Frank Warren, the London promoter. I sat alongside him and he said Frank was arranging a press conference in London with the American Showtime television executive Jay Larkin, and Joe Calzaghe who had been boxing, defending his world title against Sakio Bika at Manchester on the Saturday night and had won on points but was given a rough ride. The driver dropped us off at the Mandarin Hotel. I enquired about the cost of a room there and it was about £500 per night so I booked into one across the road for half the price. I bumped into Pierce Brosnan in the Mandarin foyer and was amazed how small he was. I told Ray I would meet up with him the following morning at the Mandarin.

I went over to the Mandarin at midday and noticed a Bentley outside with F1 on the plate which I took to be Frank Warren's. The press conference was being held on the lower floor and I introduced myself to the security guy and he let me in without any problem. Ray was at the top table with Warren, Larkin, Calzaghe and a few others whom I didn't know. The room was full of journalists including Colin Hart and Brian Doogan. Joe

Calzaghe was sporting a swollen eye from his fight the night before. They spoke about the fight and also announced that they were bringing the Contender boxing programme here with a USA v UK team. After the conference I mingled with the journalists and introduced myself to Frank Warren. Frank was very nice and said that he thought they were great tours that I was organising and great for the British fight fans.

We were picked up at 3pm and driven to Gatwick to meet up with Lee Greenwood the next show promoter. Lee was a large guy who also ran an Amateur club and said he was putting a few bouts on at the dinner. Lee asked if I could get Ray down to the VIP area for 6.30 for the photo session. The session went ok then Ray went back to his room to rest. Emily asked me if I would sit next to Ray on the top table when he came into the room. Terry Marsh was on the other side of me whom I had a good chat and laugh with as Terry had a unique sense of humour. Barry McGuigan's son Shane boxed on the bill and looked very good in outpointing his opponent. Richie Woodhall and Clinton McKenzie also attended the event; and Clinton had boxed Ray as an Amateur in the 1976 Montreal Olympic games where Ray won the gold medal.

The following morning I had a stroll on the golf course with Lee and we spoke at length about the Amateur game. Lee drove us to Gatwick airport where we took our short flight to Manchester to meet up with John H Stracey who was staging the next show at Liverpool.

John was a great guy whom I had a lot of time for as he was a champion when I first got into boxing and he was also the first speaker I had ever featured. John picked us up at 5.15pm and we set off for the one hour drive to Liverpool's Devonshire Hotel.

The Devonshire Hotel was only a 3 star hotel and I could foresee problems somehow as my room had a strange smell to it and Emily said her room also did, but we had a good laugh about it. John wanted Ray down as soon as possible to sign items and pose for photos with fans. I knew this would be a bit of a push and Ray wasn't too happy about it but eventually we came to an agreement and Ray did his best. In the meantime I also got a call from Ray Fisher who was helping promote the Dublin show and he also wanted to get some items signed. This became a nightmare, as it was John's show and he did not want Ray to give any of his time up for anyone else's show, but somehow I managed to sit with Ray and explain it to him, that once he had signed the items it would save him doing them in Dublin.

I brought Ray down into the VIP area where he posed for photos with former champions Robbie Davies, Jimmy Price and Joey Singleton; this seemed to go on forever but Ray was ok with it. Ray then asked if he could go for his meal in private.

Kathy Stracey took us into the room to the national anthem and I sat next to Colin Hart and Kathy. Kathy was a laugh and had her elderly mother helping to sell the raffle tickets. After the introductions Ray was brought into the room to the Contender theme music and looked class. Emily came over to me and asked if I had checked my email to which I replied no. She said could I please do it as Elliott Kleinberg had sent a message. I checked this immediately and the message from Elliott was one of complaint about the substandard hotel. So either Ray or Emily must have complained back to Elliott. The problem was that it was too late now. I relayed the message to John but the show was over and we could hardly change hotels now. John mentioned to me that Tony Blair had once stayed at the hotel in the same room that Ray had occupied.

The following morning John H Stracey sorted our travel to Manchester airport for our flight to Gatwick where we were due to meet up with Mark Peters' staff. Emily was not too happy that we could not get three seats together on the plane but I said the flight was only about 30 minutes so just please bear with it.

We were picked up by Richard who worked for Mark Peters and was very professional. The journey to Stockbrook Manor was quite long and I had to change seats as I felt sick travelling the wrong way. At the Manor, which was very luxurious, they mixed up and put me in the best room so I called Ray and took a look at his and then showed him mine, and then we swapped over as it was a room fit for a king, although Ray was not too bothered.

At each hotel we went to, once I had unpacked I would put whatever suit and shirt I was going to wear over the bath rail and run the bath so that the steam took all of the creases out of them. I did this at the Manor and after having a stroll out on the golf course I returned to my room to find my suit trousers had slid off the rail and were lying in the bath full of hot water. Luckily I had another suit with me but I took the trousers down to reception to ask if I could have them dried and the girls had a good laugh after I explained what had happened to them. They said it would be tomorrow before they could have them dried, which was fine by me.

Mark Peters' driver Richard turned up with Dave Boy Green who asked me if he could go and pick Ray up when he was ready to go to the function and surprise him by knocking on his room door.

Ray came down with Dave and Richard drove us to the venue. Ray did the photos with the VIPs first and then we went into the function room. Mark had set up half of a boxing ring on the top table which looked excellent. I sat next to Ray and Terry Marsh was on the other side of me. They played the British national anthem and Terry Marsh remained seated all the way through. I nudged Ray and we had a laugh about it as he wondered why Terry would not stand up, but Terry had his own personal reasons for this – he whispered something to me about spending ten months in prison at her Majesty's service. The dinner took ages to serve but I chatted with Ray and as we were on the same wavelength it was all good crack. Ray did about 30 minutes of questions and answers and this went well. He stayed for another few photos with fans and then we left at midnight. Ray called to my room saying he had lost his phone but then I got in touch with Emily and found out that she had it. We agreed to meet at 10am on Thursday October 19th to go to London for the Mark Peters show there.

The drive to London took about an hour and a half and I sat

facing Ray and Emily but as I was going the wrong way I felt sick again and Ray must have noticed this and asked me if I was ok, I told him it was because I was facing the wrong way and he laughed and swapped seats with me and when I asked him how he could travel like that he said it was because he was tough! And we had a good laugh about it.

We arrived at the plush London Marriott hotel and after lunch I went and checked my bank account to find out that one of the promoters' cheques had bounced – just what you need especially, after they had had their show. I called him but got no reply, so this was something I would have to chase up along the way. This show was Mark Peters' show so I knew everything would be done to perfection. Emily had a couple of the Contender show winners there for photos to help promote the show over here. Steve Bunce, the boxing journalist, rang me and asked if Ray would do a piece on his show, but I just passed him over to Emily who was very professional at her job. I sat next to Ray at the top table with Charlie Magri on the other side of me. In the audience were some of the star top footballers namely John Terry, Jamie Redknapp and also the actor Ray Winstone who were all boxing fans. Mark introduced me to them along with Ray and we had our photos taken in a private area. At the dinner the auction was going very well and I noticed that a certain blonde on one of the front tables was bidding and then pulling out at the last minute. I pointed this out to Ray and he said he had also noticed it and we both had a laugh about her, but she did it repeatedly so someone had obviously planted her to get the bid up.

I had to contact Dave Furnish from Cardiff who was the next show promoter as Emily had told me that Elliott Kleinberg had checked out the Cardiff hotel and found out it was only listed as a two star. I tried to explain that I had stayed at that hotel before with Roberto Duran and it was fine, but they would have none of it and asked to be moved to a four star hotel. I felt sorry for Dave as he was a real genuine guy. I met up with an old pal from Jarrow, Kevin Chambers, at the London show and he said he was now into White Collar Boxing which was basically unlicensed.

The following morning we were due to be picked up for the Cardiff show at 1pm. The car arrived but it was just a car and there was no way we could get all of our luggage into the boot, so I called Dave Furnish and explained this to him and he said he would try and organise a people carrier. After about an hour a carrier turned up and we got settled for the trip to Cardiff. The traffic into Cardiff was jammed and we were then informed that the Welsh singer Tom Jones was performing that night at a venue which was right nearby our hotel. As we eventually arrived at the hotel Joe Egan turned up with his brother and asked for a few photos but could see we were now pushed for time.

Dave Furnish's son picked us up at about 8.45pm and that would mean we could go straight into the venue as the dinner would be over. At the venue, St Peters Hall, I sat alongside Ray and Eddie Avoth a former Welsh champion who smoked a big cigar. Ray spoke behind a lectern and told more stories here than at other venues; he was a class act. The photo session was going fine until Les Clark's batteries ran out but he quickly got them sorted to keep everybody happy. We were back at the hotel for midnight and all had gone well.

Dave Furnish arrived at the hotel at 9am with more posters for Ray to sign but Ray was fine with them and had taken a liking to Dave. Big Joe Egan came with us to the airport for our flight to Dublin at 11.15am. The flight was only about 45 minutes and when we arrived at Dublin Airport there were press everywhere. Big Joe had set this up and loved the limelight and being with the champions, but was also great company and a real character. Joe had a Hummer limousine pick us up and gave us a running commentary as we went along our way to the hotel. In the Hummer Ray got his DVD out and showed us all clips of his 50th birthday party and his house and kids. On the way Joe decided that it might be a good idea to go and visit his mother and her pals as they lived in elderly accommodation not far from where we were. Apparently Mike Tyson had also been here on his visit. Joe's mother was ecstatic at meeting Ray in her very small place and as we chatted for a few minutes quite a few of her pals also came out to meet Ray. Ray was fine with this but I was getting constant calls from the joint promoter Ray Fisher asking where the hell we were.

We eventually arrived at the hotel and one of Ray Fisher's staff turned up with a box of photos for Ray to sign. Ray Fisher said the top Irish boxing journalist Jimmy Magee was wanting to do a quick radio interview with Ray and had everything set up for this. I contacted Emily for her to inform Ray and she was fine by it but did not know what room Ray was in and he was not answering his phone. This type of thing happened quite often on tours as I found with all of the champions – they only did what they wanted to do and when they wanted to do it. Ray Fisher was not happy with all of these media guys getting their piece and eventually said Ray had to be taken to the function room now as there were people waiting to have their photos with him. The photo shoot was very disorganised with people coming from all angles and about three different photographers. As it was going on too long a guy started to ring a bell to get us all into the function room and he was doing it repeatedly, so much that it was driving us all mad, especially Emily.

At the dinner we were all walked into the room to the Rocky theme music which was a little old hat but whatever. I sat on the top table next to Emily and Joe Egan and Ray sat next to Barry McGuigan. After the meal they had an auction then Jimmy Magee interviewed Barry McGuigan, then Jim Rock, then Bernard Dunne and then eventually Ray. There were no questions from the audience. Barry McGuigan sang Danny Boy as his father used to before his fights and Barry was actually quite good. I then had a drink in the bar afterwards with Mark Peters, as it happened to be his birthday that day, and then Ray Fisher and his wife came in and we sat chatting until the early hours.

Ray Fisher had organised another function at a small place called Sligo which was apparently only a couple of hours' drive away. We were getting picked up to go to Sligo at 1.30pm to go to Mick and Maureen Kane's bar at Sligo; apparently Mick was a wealthy guy and had also had Mike Tyson visit his pub. Ray came downstairs to the restaurant area and we sat and had a cheeseburger each. Scott Welsh, Emily and Tony and Shane the security lads were already seated having breakfast. As we had a couple of hours to spare and it was a beautiful day the security guys Shane and Tony took us for a stroll along Dublin's famous O'Connell Street. Emily wanted a picture of the statue of Molly Malone and was fascinated by the story which I told her about through the words of the song which I knew very well. We then visited Dublin University and Ray picked up a few items for his kids.

I travelled to Sligo in a Range Rover with security and Ray and Emily travelled in a Bentley. On arrival at Mick Kane's pub in Sligo there were hundreds of kids outside, some of them in their Amateur boxing strips with their coaches. We arrived first and then when Ray arrived they had a police Garda escort vehicle which sounded the sirens as they drove in.

The kids screamed and cheered as Ray got out of the car and he immediately posed for photos with the kids and signed autographs. Inside the pub it was packed with locals and Ray asked if he could go upstairs for a rest after the long drive which had been tiring. I had a drink with Ray Fisher and mingled with the locals. Ray came down after about an hour or so and came into a small lounge where a few Irish guys were playing a fiddle and a flute. They asked Ray to sit with them and gave him a turn at playing the flute. Ray blew into it but no sound came out and they all had a good laugh about it.

Mick told us that he had arranged a small dinner upstairs in his pub for about 7.30pm. There were only about 50 people there as it was only a small room but I sat at the front table alongside Jimmy White the snooker player, with Ray and Emily alongside me. Steve Collins, Scott Welsh Joe Egan, Tommy Scragg and Mark Peters were also on the table. Mark Peters MC'd the evening and also sang a few songs and was very good doing his version of a Tom Jones classic. Joe Egan's wife Ruth got Ray up onto the dance floor and he moved with rhythm even when on the dance floor. We had a really good relaxing night to end the tour.

I got in the car with Ray Fisher and his charming wife to head back to the hotel at Dublin and then we all had a drink together in the bar and said our farewells.

Ray, Emily and I were taken by Security to Dublin Airport at 9am and we were all ready for home. Ray spotted that we could get an earlier flight to Heathrow which I checked on and the girl said yes you can but it will cost you £275 so I had to get it. Ray also noticed that there was a flight on the board which went to Los Angeles and said he would have to get this sorted next time but what he did not realise was that that flight was going to Paris first and then LA so decided to go to Heathrow with me.

We arrived at Heathrow at midday and then all said our farewells as I left them at the lift for terminal 3 and I took a flight to Newcastle.

Once again, although it was a huge relief when the tour was over, I had a fantastic time travelling with arguably the greatest boxer of all time in Ray Leonard and mixing with some great champions and characters from the world of boxing.

It was after these tours with Thomas Hearns and Ray Leonard that some of the newer promoters asked me if I could organise another tour with Roberto Duran.

MARTYN, RAY LEONARD & ACTOR RAY WINSTONE, LONDON, 2006

MARTYN AND MARK PETERS (MC & PROMOTER), LONDON, 2006

THE FINAL ROUND

I first met Mark Peters at a show Roberto Duran attended in Peterborough for Kevin Sanders. I recall Mark coming over to me, telling me he was the comedian for the show and asking me if I thought Roberto would be offended as during his act he stripped off and wore just a fig leaf. I informed Roberto and he just laughed and I recall that Mark was actually quite entertaining. Since then Mark had branched out and apart from becoming a very good MC he also provided PA systems and had also started promoting his own shows. It was Mark who pushed me into organising another tour for Robert, as he said that he would personally like to stage two shows down in the South. I knew I could do a show up here and I would advertise for another couple. Although we had not left on the best of terms after the last tour I contacted Tony Gonzalez and he said he would love to come over and tour again with Roberto.

Dave Furnish from Cardiff contacted me and said he would do another show with Roberto, and Dave was a man of his word, and a new promoter Keith Mayo from the Swindon area said he would like to feature Roberto. I then received calls from John H Stracey and Wally Dixon to stage shows and this would complete a tour for one week during early October 2007.

As a Friday night was always a good night for shows I decided to start the tour off at the Quayside Exchange buildings in Sunderland. To help sell the show I kept the tickets prices rock bottom and also added that there would be a surprise guest appearing. I contacted one of Roberto's previous opponents, Jimmy Batten, whom Roberto had fought in Miami. I had met Jimmy at previous shows and found him to be a real nice guy who was great to talk to and also liked to sing a song. I thought it a good idea to get Jimmy to come along and meet up with Roberto again and he could also sing a few songs to provide the evening's entertainment.

I contacted Sandra, manageress at the Quality Hotel where Roberto had stayed on his previous visit to Sunderland, and asked Sandra to book rooms for Roberto, Tony and Jimmy. I received an email from Tony saying their flight, due in at 12.30, was delayed and would now not be in until 13.39 which meant another hour hanging around the airport.

I spotted Roberto first dressed in a black polo neck jumper and black trousers. He immediately waved to me and then came over and gave me one of his bear like hugs and handshakes; Tony did likewise. I drove them over to the hotel in my own car. At the hotel I noticed Roberto was limping quite badly. When I asked what had happened he said he had fallen off his motorcycle and hurt his knee. I let them settle in their rooms and then received a call from Jimmy Batten to say he was already in the hotel. I went along to see Jimmy and had a good chat with him and let him know what time he would be picked up for the show. I then went back to see Roberto and asked him to sign the gloves and items for the show.

I found it was always best to put the signings deal within the contract so that there were no arguments over what and how many items were to be signed, and that any extra would mean extra payment too.

My driver Alan 'Dobba' Dobson dropped Roberto and Tony off right on time and Roberto had the audience laughing as he entered the room wearing dark glasses pretending to be blind and staggering about. The question and answer session was very good and Roberto and Tony always responded well between them and never ducked any questions. Jimmy Batten also spoke well and sang a few songs at the end of the evening whilst Roberto posed for photos with fans.

Jimmy Batten asked me if it would ok if he sold a few DVDs of his fight with Roberto. I told Jimmy I had no problem with this and would look forward to watching it myself as I recall when the fight happened it was one of the support bouts for the Alexis Arguello v Aaron Pryor title bout and was not televised as most people had left the arena.

The Sunderland area has always produced some good boxers and they were all out in force at the show and one of the former boxers, big Andy Parkin who now ran a successful debt collecting agency, had organised to take a table with a lot of the lads on who all had some great banter with Roberto. One of the boxers on their table was Gordon 'Pedro' Phillips, who was one of the best boxers to come out of Sunderland and always went far in the ABA finals. I recall going down to London to watch Gordon box Rod Douglas in the 1985 ABA finals in which he put up a terrific performance only to lose out on points.

On the way back to the hotel Tony asked me if there was anywhere open that we could get a transformer for his laptop and also some medication for Roberto's knee. The hotel was close to an Asda store which is open 24 hours so we pulled in there. The time was midnight and the store was quiet with few people about. Roberto went straight over to the sandwiches and also picked up some milk, but all we could get was some deep heat cream for his knee problem. It felt strange that we usually did our weekend shopping at this Asda and here I was in at midnight with one of the greatest boxers of all time.

The following morning we drove to Newcastle Central station where we took the train journey to London to be picked up for the next show at Swindon.

I always booked first class seats with a table if possible. As we took our seats at the table Tony said to me that Roberto had said he liked travelling on trains and knew he would be on them when on tour with Martyn. It was always my preferred way of travel over here on longer journeys as you had room to move and not the hassle of queues and searches at airports, and could also get into the city centres a lot easier.

I sat alongside Jimmy and I asked if he wanted to play his bout with Roberto on my laptop as I would like to see it, so Jimmy kindly put it on. Roberto and Tony watched the fight for a few rounds but then Roberto appeared to be bored and closed his eyes. Jimmy said isn't it unbelievable that today I am sitting on a train with Roberto watching our bout from all those years ago that was the biggest bout of my life and what people mainly knew me for, but it obviously didn't mean that much to Roberto as he dozed off after watching a few rounds. As we approached London Roberto then realised that he had left his jacket at the hotel in Sunderland, and asked me if I could get it for him. I rang the hotel and also Dobba to make arrangements for him to pick it up and try and come down to one of the shows. Dobba actually had a few contacts in the Manchester area so said he would make arrangements to come down there to the show on Wednesday with Roberto's jacket.

As Roberto and Tony had no phones with them Tony asked if he could make a call from my mobile. I immediately thought about the cost of phoning Miami or Panama from my mobile, but I could hardly refuse.

With the second show booked for the Saturday at Swindon and the next show on the Tuesday at Liverpool it meant I had to accommodate Roberto and Tony for the Sunday and Monday nights.

I thought about contacting Joe Pyle again but then thought that might be a bit cheeky so I contacted a smashing guy whom I had met several times at various shows, Big Joe Egan. Joe was a former sparring partner to Mike Tyson and was well known in the boxing circles on the celebrity dinner circuit. I mentioned this to Joe and he said that he would be more than happy to accommodate Roberto in the Birmingham area for a couple of nights where he was based. Joe was a larger than life character, probably about 6' 3" and weighing in at super heavyweight, although he always looked fit as a fiddle with his rosy cheeks and fresh complexion. I did warn Joe not to organise any private shows at which there was money handed over as Roberto and Tony would catch onto this and ask for their cut.

At King's Cross rail station we were met by Bernard Micallef, a cousin of former world flyweight champion Charlie Magri. Bernard had organised the transport to take us to Swindon which was about a two hour drive. The transport was a luxurious black people carrier.

The drive to Swindon was a little longer than expected due to the London traffic. During the journey Joe Egan was ringing me constantly to make sure everything was ok. I said to Joe that I had informed Tony about him and that all should be ok, but you could never guarantee anything with Roberto.

At Swindon we were met by the promoter and businessman Keith Mayo, a nice guy who ran a large garage MOT station and was very well known in the area. I had asked Keith to try and get us all on the ground floor of the hotel due to Roberto's knee problem and he did oblige my request.

Bernard asked us to be ready for 7pm to be picked up to go to the venue which was a ten minute drive away from the hotel. As usual Roberto was not ready and when he did eventually come out of his room he decided he wanted a coffee.

At the venue we were taken into a large marquee first and Roberto had photos taken by Alan Shaw with VIP guests. Alan Shaw appeared on the boxing dinner circuit from time to time and he always had a go at me for not using him at my own shows, but I used to have a laugh with him and tell him I used a proper photographer – it was all in good fun and I found Alan to be a great guy and very accommodating at photo sessions. Alan had apparently been a member of a well known pop group in the 70s. Roberto noticed there was a pool table in the bar area and asked the guy who was playing if he could join in. Roberto was quite a good player and the guy was made up playing against him but they could not finish the game as we were called into the main room for dinner.

On the top table there was Mark Peters who was MC for the show, and me, Tony, Roberto and Jimmy Batten. Mark showed some big screen fight clips of Roberto and introduced him to great applause. Questions from the audience came and then out of the blue Mark fired a question to me at the top table asking what it was like to be in Roberto's company. Although unprepared for a question I just said that it was a great experience and that Tony and Roberto were like a double comedy act as they were always laughing, joking and carrying on with each other. I also announced for us all to congratulate Tony on the birth of his son a few weeks earlier. Roberto's daughter Irichelle was the mother of the child and imagine having Roberto for a father in law? A member of the audience asked Roberto if it was true that he once kept a lion as a pet. Roberto said yes, it was true, and started to tell the story which Tony translated for him. Roberto got up out of his seat and stood at the front of the stage as he told the story.

Apparently several years ago a circus came to Panama and when they were due to leave there must have been some problems with the cost and a lot of red tape involved in taking the animals from one country to another, so the circus decided to sell some of the animals off to the locals and Roberto chose to buy himself a pet young lion.

Roberto told the audience that he would take it out for a walk around Panama on a lead. He then went on to tell them about how he used to go out into his back garden and wash the lion down with a hose. He had the audience in howls of laughter when he told them how the lion would stand with its two front legs on a table and Roberto would get the soap and build up a lather and wash him down, starting at the top and working his way down the lion's back and stomach area. Then when he got down to its private parts the lion would give a great roar of pleasure. The way Roberto described this standing on the stage was absolutely hilarious, and the tears were rolling down my face for about ten minutes after he'd finished. I still laugh now when I think of it. He went on to say that every time Roberto went out into his garden the lion would rush over and put its front legs up on the table, hoping it was going to get a hose down again. He told the audience that the lion eventually died.

After the show I spoke with Tony and said that I had made arrangements for us all to go to Birmingham tomorrow, Sunday, and that we would be looked after and I would also get them a payment for some signings that Joe Egan had organised, but Tony said Roberto wanted to go to Disneyland Paris and asked if I could book a taxi to take them to Heathrow Airport early in the morning.

This all came as a surprise to me as I had arranged with Joe Egan to sort something out for the Sunday and Monday which Joe had obligingly done and now he would not be too happy that Roberto had changed his mind. I tried and tried and asked Tony and Roberto to change their minds but they were adamant that they wanted to go to Paris. I felt bad about this but rang Joe and explained it to him as best I could; he was none too happy about it, but what could I do?

I had two days to kill now until the next show at Liverpool on Tuesday so I asked about Swindon and found out that there was not that much there so decided I would make my way to Liverpool instead, which was always a bustling city and had recently been awarded European capital of culture. A train journey would have meant changing at different stations a couple of times and as it was a Sunday the trains were not frequent so I decided that the best deal would be from a cab company and to be driven there directly in under three hours.

I arrived in Liverpool late on Sunday afternoon and sorted accommodation in the city centre and did a tour of the pubs including the famous Cavern pub and club where the Beatles had played. The pubs were all busy and most had sing alongs and Karaoke going on. With Liverpool winning the capital of culture award there was a lot of building work going on all over the city so you were constantly ducking in and out of scaffolding around the city centre area, but I'll bet it would have been worth a visit on completion.

Tony contacted me on the Monday evening to say that they

would be arriving back from Paris at Manchester airport at 4pm but he was not sure of the terminal. I said I would find out and meet him there.

Manchester Airport is absolutely massive and I discovered that the flights from Paris arrived at similar times, around 4pm, but they arrived at three different terminals. It was a complete headache trying to find out which one they would be arriving at so I just went to one of them and then awaited a call from Tony letting me know where he was – sure enough he was at T1, furthest away from me at T3.

I eventually met up with them and we took a cab to Liverpool. The time was now 5.30pm and John H Stracey, who was running the Liverpool show, had asked me to try and get Roberto there for 6pm so that he could sign the memorabilia items before the show for him. We arrived at about 6.30pm and John was not too happy but at least we were there.

As John H was rushing trying to get our rooms sorted and Roberto ready for the show my phone rang and it was Roberto's wife, Fula, on the line.

I had previously met Fula on my stay in Panama and she was still very smart. Fula spoke quite good English and was asking if everything was ok and then asked if she could speak to Roberto. Roberto took the call sitting on the corner of his bed in his underwear as he was awaiting his shirt and trousers being ironed. Tony asked if I could get an iron from reception for him. The hotel staff brought an iron up immediately and John H Stracey started ironing Roberto's shirt. I don't know what he was saying but Roberto and Fula appeared to be having a domestic as he was screaming down the phone, but Tony just continued getting ready and was just laughing and said, "Don't worry about it – I hear it all the time."

John H Stracey had the photo session organised before we went into the main room but there appeared to be hundreds awaiting photos. The session went ok and we then were all taken into the main room to a fanfare and introduced to the audience. I sat alongside Phil, a property developer and one of the main sponsors for John H Stracey. Once we were settled Roberto and Tony asked if they could eat in private and went off into a small back room. During the dinner most of the promoters shows clips of Roberto's fights on the big screen so he really didn't need to be there until the question and answer session.

Tony and Roberto came back through to rapturous applause and handled the questions well. I set one of the guys in the audience up to ask Roberto about his pet lion and told him he would get a good laugh about it and sure enough Roberto told the tale over again and had them all in stitches of laughter. At the end of the evening Roberto retired to his room and I had a few drinks with Tony Gonzalez and David Walker, who was a representative for the WBC belts.

The next morning I had repeated calls from Big Joe Egan saying he was on his way to Liverpool with the next show's promoter, Wally Dixon, and wanted me to do a favour for him.

Joe said that because he had been put in an embarrassing situation with Roberto not going to Birmingham, would it be possible to save face for him if on the way to Manchester we could drop in to meet some of Joe's friends on the way. I said that it should not be a problem if it was on the way; Joe said it would only be a short detour.

John H rang me at 9.30am and asked if before we went to Manchester he wanted Roberto to sign some gloves for him. I called Tony and he said he would wake Roberto and give me a call when he was ready.

Also at 9.30am big Joe Egan and Wally Dixon turned up at the hotel along with another car driven by Lee, their security guy. Joe asked if I could get Roberto up and ready as soon as possible so that we could get on our way to Manchester which was only about an hour's drive away but he wanted to drop into his friend's pub on the way.

Roberto eventually rose and signed John H Stracey's items for him but then asked if he could have some breakfast. As the hotel breakfasts were now finished Big Joe said that he would get Roberto something to eat on the motorway on our way to

Manchester.

Joe was driving a massive Range Rover jeep and his security guy Lee was in a Mercedes. Joe asked Roberto and Tony to travel in the Mercedes and Wally Dixon and I travelled with Joe in the Jeep.

We set off and Joe was speeding down the motorway to wherever his pal's pub was. After about half an hour Lee rang Joe and said Roberto was asking for something to eat. Joe replied saying to tell him to wait a little while as we were not too far away from the pub and he could get something to eat there.

This went on for another half-hour and Wally started panicking thinking that if we unsettled Roberto it would spoil his show for him, but Joe was adamant that he had to get Roberto to his pal's pub to save face for Roberto not going there earlier as he, Joe, had promised.

Lee, the driver behind, was also panicking saying that Roberto wanted to speak to Martyn. I took the call and Joe asked me to insist to him that we were only ten minutes away from stopping. Joe then said that he had a few newspaper guys at the pub and would Roberto be ok for a few photos, but Wally said that Roberto would smell a rat and he did not want this to affect his show at Manchester tonight.

Joe was driving at high speeds and kept saying we were only minutes away but the short detour was tuning into an hour and a half drive and Roberto and Tony were now getting very agitated.

We eventually pulled up at a pub somewhere near Wolverhampton and there were about 30 rough looking guys outside.

One of the guys had some harsh words with Wally and Joe, but we then went into the pub and were offered sandwiches and drinks. I could tell Roberto was uneasy and so was I, so suggested to Joe that it would be best if we did not stay too long. Roberto only had a small snack and posed for a couple of photos, one of which was with the 82 year old landlady of the pub. Wally suggested we get back on the road to Manchester as he had things to do for his show; Joe wasn't too happy about this but we had to keep Roberto sweet as the last thing you needed would be for him to pull out of the show.

We went straight back on the road and Joe said he would stop at the nearest service station and get Roberto something decent to eat. We did this just a few miles on and Joe cheered Roberto up with some food and jokes. I apologised to Roberto and he appeared to be ok so we drove on to the Piccadilly Hotel at Manchester for Wally's show. At the Piccadilly we checked in and Wally told us that we had to meet at 6.30pm for photos. At the photo shoot all of the regular champions were present: Alan Minter, Ken Buchanan, Earnie Shavers, Joe Egan, Brian London. Ken Buchanan had a few drinks and started causing the photographer a few problems, messing about. Just then I got a call from Dobba saying that he had arrived with the jacket that Roberto had left in Sunderland. I explained to Wally about the jacket and Dobba and his pal had their photo with Roberto and the champions as they had travelled a long way and it was very kind of them.

We went through into the function room where about 350 dinners were waiting to see Roberto. Ricky Hatton turned up with Paul Speak and sat alongside Roberto and discussed a few of his fights that were being shown on the big screen during the dinner. The show was ok but once again the auction ran on far too long; however Mark Peters handled it as professionally as ever, and Ray Lewis from the Drifters performed some excellent old songs that had the audience singing along. Roberto only signed a few items as he was really tired and we all went back to our rooms at about midnight.

The next show was in Essex with Mark Peters promoting so I booked our train tickets for me, Roberto and Tony from Manchester to Euston. Mark Peters rang me to make sure that Ken Buchanan had got the train, and then Wally Dixon rang to make sure his nine items had been signed by Roberto, I told him that I did not have the items and he said he would send his driver Lee to London with them.

I booked first class seats on the Virgin train to London and I sat and chatted with Jimmy Batten who was also travelling to the show. Roberto slept and Tony watched one of his DVDs which must have been hilarious as he laughed continuously all the way to London.

We were picked up at London in a massive Hummer limousine, but it was a two hour drive to our hotel in Essex. Roberto was in a plush suite downstairs. We were being picked up again at 6.30 in the Hummer and taken to a posh venue called the Boathouse where the function was being held.

We were taken through to the photo shoot area first which was handled by my old pal Alan Shaw. I joked with him and asked why he was using a dust sheet for his background scenery, which we had a good laugh about and he said he would keep his best dust sheet for my shows when I would book him. Ken Buchanan started messing about again at the photos and his agent had to take him away for a walk. We were then taken into the food area where we sat at a corner table and I sat alongside my old pal, former world champion Colin McMillan, whose company I always enjoyed and had a good chat with. We appeared to wait for ages before we were served but when I mentioned it to Mark Peters he got things moving immediately. During the meal Mark Peters had set up a Salsa band to play and Roberto appeared to enjoy this. A small stage was set up for Roberto and Tony although Jimmy Batten was up first and handled the questions well but was given the wrong microphone and could hardly be heard. Mark sorted this out and then started the auction which pulled in unbelievable money in comparison to the North East of England. Roberto and Tony then took the stage and handled the same old questions well. During the questions I met up with one of Freddie Foreman's pals whom I had met when with Joe Pyle and had a good long chat with him. After the show the Hummer took us to a club called Talk Talk which was full of youngsters but the management guys came and took us to a VIP area which was a lot better and we all had a laugh at Roberto's antics, larking about. We stopped off on the way back at a carry out and all got chicken and chips.

The next show was also with Mark Peters promoting in central London, so we were due to be picked up at 9.30am by Brian, Mark's driver. Brian was spot on time as usual but Roberto and Tony were not ready until 10.00...as usual.

The drive to London took longer than expected due to a lorry breakdown but Brian showed us a few of the sights as we travelled across the city. At the hotel which was the Hilton Metropole we had to wait until 2pm before we could get into our rooms, but the owner came over to us and served us coffee and snacks.

I received a call from Wally Dixon's driver Lee to say that he had set off for London and would call me when he arrived to have his items signed. I also had a call from John H Stracey saying he would be coming to the hotel to have a few items signed. All of this signing stuff was becoming a proper pain.

We were due to be picked up at 6pm. The limousine arrived for us all. Ken Buchanan and his agent, Jimmy Batten and Steve Collins also turned up and was always a laugh, but once again we had to await Roberto and Tony.

The function was at a place called the Brewery and was a massive old style function hall. Mark Peters first of all had to have some extra items signed by Roberto and then we went into a private area in the function room where the photo shoot began and lasted for over an hour.

Roberto sat through the meal but he had already eaten earlier. I spotted Terry Marsh in the audience and went over for a chat with him. Terry was a proper character and was undefeated as a world champion but best known for being held for the shooting of Frank Warren, for which he was eventually acquitted. The auction started and once again pulled in a lot more than you would ever get up North.

We all travelled back to the hotel in the limo but had to pull up as Ken Buchanan was sick. We all got out until Ken sorted himself out and then headed back to the hotel where I had a drink with Jimmy Batten and his girlfriend.

I got a call at my hotel room from Brian the limo driver

asking for me to get 20 photos signed by Roberto as this had apparently been arranged with Tony.

After breakfast Tony Gonzalez came over and said Lee had turned up at hotel with Wally's items to be signed and Roberto had done them so gave the bag to me to pass on.

The next show was with Dave Furnish in Cardiff and we were due to be picked up at 11.15 to catch the 11.45 train from Paddington to Cardiff. At the station we lost Tony and panicked but suddenly Roberto spotted him on the train and said Tony was crazy. On the train I sat next to Roberto and put a DVD on called 100 Knock Outs and Roberto watched it with me and got very excited watching them, clapping his hands at some of the footage.

We arrived in Cardiff a little earlier than expected and there was no one there to pick us up. I rang the organiser Dave Furnish who said he could not get there for another half hour which surprised me as Dave was usually very organised. Tony suggested we should just get a taxi to the hotel, which was the Holiday Inn where we had stayed previously.

At the hotel I received a call from Fula in Panama, but I had to tell her Roberto had gone shopping and I would call her back when he returned. I met up with Dave Furnish, a smashing guy who gave me his ten items for Roberto to sign. I gave Roberto a knock and he eventually opened the door once he knew who it was. I first of all gave him my phone to call Fula. He was not on the phone for too long and then he signed the items for Dave and I told him to be ready for 8.30 for our taxi to take us to the show.

Dave's son picked us up. I asked him if he was coming to the dinner but he said no as he wasn't really interested in them. The function was held at St Peters Hall. Dave used this venue for all of his shows and I had brought Roberto here a few years previously. A few security guys took us all upstairs into the photo shoot room where the photographer Les Clark was waiting. I had met Les before and he worked with Dave at most of his functions. Dave brought former middleweight world champion Iran Barkley through into the hall. Iran Barkley was a massive guy who had fought Roberto in a classic fight that Roberto won. They posed for a few photos. We were then introduced to the audience in the main hall by Welsh BBBC referee Wynford Jones who gave me an excellent introduction for bringing world boxing legends to Cardiff which was nice of him.

At the top table I sat next to former world featherweight champion Steve Robinson who was a nice guy and told me he was now a personal trainer and was also helping out young boxers. Steve had won his title from Newcastle's John Davison but lost it to Prince Naseem Hamed. When Roberto was introduced he came in and sat alongside me and Tony sat next to Barkley. This also happened in London when Buchanan was there.

Steve Holdsworth made his own introductions and said to the audience that he would only be taking four questions from them which I found a bit strange, but did not know what had been previously arranged with Dave Furnish. Roberto had the audience in hysterics with his tales of the circus lion story and another about the girlfriend who had made him feel good with her real heavy breathing but later found out that she had asthma.

We were then taken upstairs for the photos but Tony said that Roberto would not be signing stuff now and only posing for photos. I found this strange and the promoter Dave Furnish was totally unhappy with this and his wife even had a go at Tony Gonzalez over it. As I was the one who had brought Roberto over I went to Tony and Roberto and said to them that this was the last show and it would be really unfair for them to do this and smoothed things over so that Roberto did start to sign photos but he would not sign gloves and other items of memorabilia which was fair enough.

As Tony wanted to be at Heathrow Airport as soon as possible, I asked Dave if he could book us some transport to leave straight after the show. Dave booked us a small luxury coach which was excellent but I wondered how much it was going to cost. The driver was fine and took us back to the hotel first to pick up our luggage and then set off for the two hour drive to Heathrow. We arrived at about 2.30am at the Comfort Hotel at

Heathrow. The driver asked me for £250 which shocked me as I was only expecting to pay about £175. I only had £220 in cash so he had no option but to accept this. We checked into our rooms and arranged to get the early morning shuttle to Heathrow at 7.30am. We had breakfast and I paid the bill. Tony then called me over and said he had made a mistake with the flight. I looked and noticed that it was Gatwick airport and not Heathrow that he had booked to depart from. Tony asked the porter how far away Gatwick was and how long it would take in a taxi. The Porter said it would only be an hour's drive and booked them a taxi. The shuttle to Heathrow pulled up outside the hotel and Tony apologised for the mix up, thanked me and we shook hands. Roberto came over and gave me his usual hug and he waved me off as I climbed aboard the shuttle.

As I travelled back home I once again felt a huge weight off my shoulders and said to myself that would be the last tour I would organise. The work involved in organising payment transactions and travel arrangements, the hassle with promoters and their payments, and then demands for signings and photos all began to become a headache. It was also pointed out to me that I was getting grey hair very quickly... however, I had been to some great places, met some fantastic people over the years, and also met and travelled with and became a friend to some of the most respected boxers in the history of the sport.

People will always ask me who, out of them all, was the best to be with, but they were all great guys in their own individual ways. As newer promoters have come on the scene I have met up again with Roberto, Thomas and Ray and they will always say to me that those first tours were the best.

*DURAN'S FORMER OPPONENT IRAN BARKLEY, MARTYN
AND ROBERTO DURAN, CARDIFF, 2007*

ROBERTO, MARTYN AND FORMER OPPONENT JIMMY BATTEN, LONDON, 2007

BIG JOE EGAN AND MARTYN

JIMMY BATTEN, KEN BUCHANAN, STEVE COLLINS & MARTYN
DEVLIN AT DURAN DINNER SHOW, LONDON, 2007

ABOUT THE AUTHOR

Martyn Devlin was born and still lives in Jarrow in the North East of England. After a long amateur boxing career Martyn turned to coaching youths and has given his time freely on three evenings per week for the past 30 years as head coach, secretary and matchmaker at the Bilton Hall ABC at Jarrow. A Joiner by trade, he works for a Technical Services team in Newcastle. He has been married to Linda for 35 years and they have one daughter, Joy.

MARTYN DEVLIN WINNING AGAINST DAVEY FLYNN, NEWCASTLE, 1976